Beyond Our Self-Image

The True Story of a Fictional Character

Previous Books:

Explore Within: A Journey to Inner Peace N.T Hettigei,
Independently Published, 2019–2022
ISBN: 9798365838635

Are You a Philosopher or a Sage? Explore Your Inner Peace N.T.
Hettigei, Independently Published, 2009
ISBN: 9781439251911

Beyond Our Self-Image

The True Story of a Fictional Character

N.T. Hettigei

BOOKS

Winchester, UK
Washington, USA

JOHN HUNT PUBLISHING

First published by O-Books, 2024
O-Books is an imprint of John Hunt Publishing Ltd., 3 East St., Alresford,
Hampshire SO24 9EE, UK
office@jhpbooks.com
www.johnhuntpublishing.com
www.o-books.com

For distributor details and how to order please visit the 'Ordering' section on our website.

Text copyright: N.T. Hettigei 2023

ISBN: 978 1 80341 474 4
978 1 80341 475 1 (ebook)
Library of Congress Control Number: 2022923038

A CIP catalogue record for this book is available from the British Library.

Design: Lapiz Digital Services

UK: Printed and bound by CPI Group (UK) Ltd, Croydon, CR0 4YY
Printed in North America by CPI GPS partners

The author of this book does not dispense medical advice or
prescribe the use of any technique as a form of treatment for
physical, emotional, or medical problems without the advice of a
physician, either directly or indirectly. The intent of the author
is only to offer information of a general nature to help you in
your quest for emotional and spiritual well-being. In the event
you use any of the information in this book for yourself, which is
your constitutional right, the author and the publisher assume no
responsibility for your actions.

We operate a distinctive and ethical publishing philosophy in
all areas of our business, from our global network of authors to
production and worldwide distribution.

Contents

"Worldly satisfaction obscures true happiness."
—N.T. Hettigei

To
My Wife,
Nadeeka

Preface

You may think that the true story of a fictional character is a contradictory and confusing statement. But once you go beyond your self-image, you realize that you have been living as a fictional character, and your true self is not who or what you thought you were!

I was compelled to write this true story of the fictional character I have lived with throughout my life. Since my childhood, I have been exploring everything inwardly and outwardly. While inwardly exploring, I realized I lived in a conceptualized self—a self-image—and I thought that was my essence. But when I realized that my true self is not who I thought I was, I began using my true self—inner peace—to navigate my life challenges rather than become a victim of my self-image.

My intention here is to share my true story and experiences with you to provide you with enough tools and references to experience your true self. You will experience your true self beyond your fictional character of the "I am," the self-image, and with that base, you can experience true happiness and live blissfully while using your mind as a useful tool.

Through diligent meditation practices, I experienced the phenomenon beyond our conceptualized self-image. This enabled me to recognize the genuine assertions made by many teachers, both in modern and in ancient times, and relate them to my own experience. I have shared this experience with others in small group settings for the last three decades. This book is my effort to help you and many others go beyond your self-image to experience true happiness and live a blissful life.

Plenty of resources point seekers in the right direction in this information age. However, many are left on the brink of transcendence to the true self because conceptual thinking keeps them at bay from the truth. I am sharing a unique and simple approach to help you resolve that gap in many spiritual and religious publications and teachings, enabling you to experience true happiness firsthand.

While this book's purpose is primarily to enhance your experience of inner peace, it also attempts to heal a world divided by petty differences, to wake up to a wiser civilization. When deeply investigated, I see true self, or true happiness, is promoted in all prevailing, peace-loving religious and spiritual teachings. Therefore, you do not have to change your faith to experience this. You will come to see all religions or faiths as the same, because every teaching points to the same truth you experience, firsthand, from practices I introduce in this book. Those teachings benefit each of us, regardless of the images we have chosen for ourselves. You will find the answer to your quest for happiness, here, if you are an open-minded seeker. During this voyage of discovery, you will learn to recognize your authentic nature—*inner peace*—and how to enrich your life and live blissfully.

You will find certain self-checks and practices to help you discover who you are and your pathway to inner peace. It will be helpful to stop reading at those places for a few minutes, and practice.

In addition, I included a few restatements, similes, and graphic representations throughout, hoping that they resonate with you and enhance your experience of true happiness. I trust that this will help you open your noble heart, or give the final push to people on the brink of transcendence to inner peace.

You may use this book as your lifestyle handbook and refer back to it. For that purpose, I included an index of practices. You may repeat any that bring you inner peace. They are *practices* rather than *exercises*. Technically, the exercises have a start and an end, but these practices are intended for constant experiences. Practice them at least twice daily, before you go to bed and when you wake up in the morning. This will elevate your inner peace and help you to experience the bliss of being alive—true happiness.

I have self-published a couple of previous books to share this experience with others, which laid the foundation for this book. If you have already read those books, including the new edition of *Explore Within,* you may find a similar message presented here but from a different perspective.

Acknowledgments

I owe plenty to others who have taught me many life lessons. This includes my fatherly brother, caring wife, and admirable daughter. It also includes the teachers of ancient religions and present-day spiritual masters.

I would like to acknowledge you, the reader, who will be interacting with me by reading this book. I sincerely believe that the information in these pages will help you live a blissful life. I acknowledge and thank you in advance for your openness, willingness to achieve your aspirations, and determination to make this world a better place. Hence, I take this opportunity to recognize your noble effort to explore within.

Further, special thanks go to my friends who reviewed and edited my original manuscript and provided valuable comments, encouraging me to improve my writing, including the late Michael Nyein of New Zealand. A similar gratitude goes to my daughter, who encouraged and inspired me to write and helped me to become a writer.

I dedicate this book to my wife, Nadeeka, who helped me navigate my life journey from the day she became a part of it. Nadee, you have been the river that allowed me to sail my lifeboat, avoiding collisions with the many challenges that came our way during our time together.

In addition, I am grateful to the professionals who helped me with editorial assessments and made copious comments and corrections through many drafts of this book.

Introduction

I consider myself an explorer because I have been exploring my surroundings and inner self since birth. Most of us are born explorers, but at an early stage of our lives, we give up exploring to pursue happiness. I have found that true happiness is the inner peace that resides in me, which is the pure alertness I was born with, and I do not doubt it. True happiness is always there for us to experience, although many people doubt this with their confusing thoughts and concepts, and live in chaos and misery.

When we are born, we are alert, full of attention, joy and happiness. You may have seen some babies born with their eyes wide open and instantly alert, wanting to see what is happening around them. You see joy and happiness in their eyes. Those babies cry only when hungry. Other babies cry as soon as they see the light of this planet, mainly because they are alert, yet terrified, to see the new world. I find that alertness is the true sense of our life that we carry into this world, which I would like to call the noble nature of our hearts. I saw it in deep meditation and realized that it's been there all along. We are all born with a noble heart; some call this consciousness, soul, inner peace, God's nature in us or, mistakenly, the mind.

If you think that you must pursue happiness, you will get lost in the ever-changing concepts. Think about what makes you unhappy. Mostly, we are unhappy because we do not have something we believe will make us happy. But once we get that thing, we may be satisfied for a few hours but then again become unhappy and decide we need something else to make us happy. In fact, it is our thoughts, perceptions, speculations, and emotions that make us unhappy. All those are created in our minds, based on our concepts. We become victims of our minds when we get lost in such thoughts, speculations, and emotions. I found a way to navigate through them and be happy without being a victim of my mind.

It is a very simple technique but hard to practice because many live in their confusing minds. I will share this simple technique and provide many examples, memoirs, and proofs, i.e., self-checks, as well as practices to enable you to clear your path to experiencing true happiness, as I constantly do. It is as simple as paying complete attention to your heart and dwelling in inner peace, free of thoughts. However, it is hard to do with our mind-created self-image. We need to open our minds to experience our true nature, the noble heart that gives us inner peace and true happiness.

My inner exploration has been ongoing since birth. Like every baby, I likely tasted dirt and many other things on the floor to know better about what they are. I did most of my inner exploration on full-moon days, sitting quietly in the corner of the hall at the village temple in Sri Lanka. It was rare for a teenager to meditate, but that was what was expected from everyone participating in such a daylong retreat. One day, while participating in a retreat, I opened my eyes after a long meditation, surprised to see many people looking at me as if they were worried I would never wake up. I would have been sitting, unmoving, in that same posture for more than two hours, but it felt like fifteen minutes or so. I am sure that you may have had similar experiences in your life, maybe when sitting on a park bench, admiring nature, or reading an interesting book, time passing without you noticing it.

In my teens, I rode my bicycle far away from the village to explore the surrounding landscape. I remember riding with my friends for twenty miles to a rubber plantation, climbing hills, spending the day examining wild plants growing under the rubber trees, and watching different types of fish colonizing the stream's stagnant water pockets. I hope you had similar childhood experiences that heightened your attention, enjoyment, and enthusiasm to explore more.

Growing up, I changed my line of study from art to science and then to commerce and economics. This was possible because of my heightened attention to things around and within me. I passed the standard tests offered by the education department on all three lines of study. Later, in my twenties, I graduated and became a chartered accountant, which I had never hoped for as a teenager. This accomplishment was a milestone in my outward exploration, aided by pure attention, developed through my inner exploration. You may have had similar accomplishments, using the heightened attention you gained in childhood, but may not have recognized it for what it was.

I migrated to New Zealand in my early thirties, and continued my internal and external expeditions. I lived in New Zealand for ten years and explored the beautiful landscape, people, and cultures there until I migrated to the USA at the end of 1999. I lived in Minneapolis, Minnesota, for fifteen years, exploring the novelty of distinct seasonal weather changes and the ups and downs that come with it. Then I moved to Phoenix, Arizona, and have lived here since.

My inner exploration took a deeper dive when I started associating with Western Buddhist monks ordained under Ajahn Cha of Thailand, who lived in the Monastery in Stokes Valley, New Zealand. I became a frequent visitor there; the monastery was four kilometers, or two and a half miles, from my home in Lower Hutt, New Zealand. I participated in long retreats and group discussions with monks and laypeople to share our knowledge and experiences. There, I learned about different Buddhist traditions and a lot more about other religions worldwide.

It was a bright summer day in 1996, and I was in a solitude retreat at that Bodhinyanarama Buddhist Monastery in Stokes Valley, when I sank deep into my noble heart. I saw myself as a fictional character created by many concepts embedded in the cognitive field, like a story written on pristine white paper. Then I transcended to total awareness and experienced, for the very first time, that I am not the one I thought I was. I saw that my inner essence was peaceful and still, and the rest was a flickering mirage outside my true self. I realized that is the true happiness we are all looking for in the midst of life's challenges. Here I am sharing that true happiness with you, in the sincere hope that you experience the same by using the practices in this book.

With that profound experience, I began to recognize the genuine assertions made by many teachers of modern and ancient times, which are identical to my own. I can relate to their approach to life and their efforts to teach others. They all promote the true happiness that I experienced, which is inner peace. I could see that many of their followers misinterpret those messages by thinking about happiness and creating their own concepts of it rather than experiencing it. That realization compelled me to share my experience with others in order to help them experience true happiness, instead of pursuing it.

I have been sharing my experience for the last three decades through in-person discussions, small group gatherings, and recently "Explore Within" biweekly workshops I conducted in Mesa, Arizona, before the pandemic. I want you to consider me a friend, sharing a way of experiencing true happiness with you. True happiness is within you to experience at will, and I trust that you will recognize it once you read and complete the practices in this book.

Once transformed by my experience, I could dwell in the present and use my intelligence more effectively to explore outwardly. I foresaw that the future of accountancy will depend on information technology, and I focused on studying and learning computer systems controls and how to audit them. While living in New Zealand, I took US certification exams and became a Certified Information Systems Auditor (CISA). After migrating to the USA, I became a Certified Public Accountant (CPA) in the State of Minnesota and later a Certified Information Systems Security Professional (CISSP). All of that was possible because I lived in my true self—inner peace—and relished true happiness, and, most importantly, I knew how to use my mind rather than be a victim of it. I can easily understand the novelty of any subject matter and get through the tests with a clear mind. Using my mind with perfect clarity also helped me easily face all life challenges, which may be troubling for many others living in their confusing minds.

These are the benefits of being in the present, or dwelling in inner peace, while also experiencing true happiness constantly. When I relate this to myself, I see that when I distance myself from my self-image—the fictional character—I transcend to inner peace and experience true happiness. I trust that you could do the same once you master the practices I introduce here.

I cannot remember what I did when I was born, but I can recall the joy and happiness I experienced as a toddler and as a child. I experience that same happiness, even now, since I came to realize that, as an adult, I was living as a fictional character enforced on me since birth. This fictional character is full of thoughts and concepts we call the mind. Now, I keep my mind at a distance and use it as a tool. I am not living in my mind but dwelling in my heart—the noble heart—experiencing true happiness. You may be doing the same without recognizing the difference between your heart and mind.

When I look at a photograph of me as a toddler, I see that I had the same smile I have today. How about you? Can you remember your childhood and the joy and happiness you experienced then? Do you carry the same happy feeling and true essence right now? My effort here is to work with you to get that happiness back so that you can live with it for the rest of your life, joyfully and blissfully. As long as you live with your self-image created by others' opinions and intellectual understanding, you deny that joyful and blissful happiness. You may think this is an impossible task. But trust me: Many people have gone beyond self-image and enjoyed true self and happiness, from ancient times to this day. You can become one of them and be part of this world, awakening to oneness.

I was a very happy boy running around in my village and treating everyone equally, and I did not know about my parents' economic and social turmoil or the rest of the world. I'm sure you had similar experiences. Can you remember them? If not, stop reading, visualize your childhood, and feel the joy and happiness running through your body and mind right now.

Although you may think that this is your memory, you are experiencing the same joy and happiness you had as a child. As I said earlier, this pleasantness or true happiness is always available for you to experience at will. The experience you just had is a good starting point for us to embark on this wondrous journey together.

On my life journey, I wonder why I have a slight smile almost all the time. There has always been an unintentional smile in me. Inadvertently, I smile at everyone, including any stranger I meet. This was probably true in my childhood as well, since I notice many children, especially in our modern era, reflect bliss with a serene smile on their eyes and faces. I realized that this smile expresses our inner peace, irrespective of our petty differences. It's like friends meeting and smiling at each other in deep-rooted friendship, without interference from the mind, our conceptualizing faculty. My heart sees inner peace in others, beyond conceptual boundaries, and I respond with a smile. Take a few seconds and contemplate a time when you smiled. It could be the very first time you met a dear friend you have now, or some stranger you never saw again after that first and only encounter. You smile at them at first sight without thinking about it, knowing nothing about them, a spontaneous smile surfaces when your inner essence touches theirs. You may agree that this is true for your current dear friend, spouse, or a soulmate, but it was also the case for the stranger you smiled at on the street. I see that deeper connection clearly, though you may not.

On a few occasions, when I smile back as a friendly gesture to people who smile at me, I read a puzzled expression that says, *Why are you smiling at me again?* Then I realize that I had unintentionally smiled at them, first, and that they responded with a smile. You may have met someone like me, or you could be someone who randomly smiles at others, too.

Once, at work, a coworker thought I was grinning at him all the time, and he kept grinning back at me like an ape encountering another ape.

This amusing incident may have brought a smile to your face. Or maybe you were offended due to speculations in your mind, thinking I am referring to an ape. Mind you, here I am referring to myself as an ape, too. I am not discriminating against anyone. I trust that this incident may have stimulated a slight blissful sensation within you, which is an expression of your inner peace. We all carry that inner peace and can elevate it to a higher degree to experience true happiness.

Therefore, this experiential journey is not a pursuit but an instant experience of true happiness—*your true self*. You may be aware by now that your pursuit of happiness will never end, since your perception of happiness always changes. Perception and mind-based pursuit is a never-ending process. When you get there, your perception will change, and you will pursue more satisfaction or happiness. Does this sound familiar? In the past, at least once, you would have deeply realized this, and that hidden realization would make you pick up this book.

We must eliminate doubt about our true nature. From my firsthand experience, I can see our true nature is inner peace, which surges out as alertness. This alertness or pure attention is the nature of our heart—the noble heart. The noble heart is not a physical organ but our essence that we access from time to time. We need to learn how to access it and dwell in it constantly to experience true happiness beyond our self-image and miseries. I will help you get there and experience it. In fact, that is the happiness you have been looking for all along.

We can eliminate doubt about ourselves to experience true happiness by answering the following four questions. I will provide answers and a few practices to enable you to experience your true self during this wondrous journey of going beyond our self-image.

Part I – Am I a Fictional Character?

This part of the book discusses our doubts about many things, including our true selves. Our true essence is not what we think we are; I am sure you already know that. Instead, you doubt my statement about the fictional character I am referring to and thereby become a victim of it. We will discuss and do a few practices to help you recognize your fictional character, your *self-image,* as apart from your true self.

Part II – What Is Our True Self?

In this part, I will work with you to identify your true self by exploring how we create our fictional characters from the moment of birth. When you were in your mother's womb, you were called "it"; after birth, some called you a baby without referring to your gender, then you were given a name, an identity, and so on. We will discuss how you built your fictional character and then do some practices to experience your essence beyond the identities given to you by others.

Part III – What Is There Beyond Self-Image?

Once you realize your true nature, you will be compelled to set aside your fictional character and go beyond it. I will help you with that in this part of the book. It may be best to use your fictional character to live in this world and create many things by using it as a tool. We will discuss how to do this effectively, without becoming a victim of this false self, by becoming a bearer of wisdom or living in true self.

Part IV – How to Experience Our True Selves?

Here, I will discuss the different approaches many teachers use to explain their experiences to others and enable you to benefit from such doctrines. I see that many methods have been used for this purpose, from ancient times to this day, and such methods are taught in our spiritual doctrines, social ethics, and other peace-loving teachings. I'll connect the dots with my experience to help you discover the path to true happiness in your faith.

For this purpose, various methods and approaches are necessary to cater to people with different temperaments and self-images. That is why different discrete groups of people accept different religions and teachings. Although the overarching temperament differs from person to person, the underlying approach to our life depends on the philosopher or sage in us. And so I see only two groups of people on this planet: some predominantly using the philosophical approach, others using the insightful approach.

You may agree with me that many of us are thinkers and philosophers. Logics, conceptual theories, and thinking dominate our minds, and we question everything until a logical answer is found. It is like a fish swimming in the ocean, looking for the so-called ocean. We lose ourselves in the ocean of concepts, boost our self-image, and never accept the fact that our essence is peaceful and universal. Instead, we may persistently challenge everything that comes from the inner self in order to achieve some form of preconceived goal or satisfaction.

This quest fades away only when we recognize that we create our world with our thoughts and perceptions, and write our own fictional characters in it. Many of us are philosophers until we cease seeking answers externally. When we realize that seeking answers or satisfaction from outside is an endless exercise, we will look inwardly and realize our true selves experientially. This is true for all of us, whether rich or poor, male or female, abled or differently abled. We must trust our noble hearts to experience our true nature beyond our self-image. In other words, any doubt leads to confusing thoughts, and clinging to self-image forbids our happiness.

I find that sages in all religions and faiths speak about the same universal state, oneness, or the noble heart common to all of us. It is not that one religion becomes the only religion in the world; instead, all human beings will recognize that, in their essence, the core doctrine of all religions is the same! You do not have to fight to protect your faith from the faith of others, since we all are practicing a universal path—*the ancient path*—to dwell in our noble heart—inner peace. We will discuss this further in the coming chapters.

In Michael A. Singer's book *The Untethered Soul: The Journey Beyond Yourself,* he states:

In the mystical Gospel of John, Christ says, "That they all may be one; as thou, Father, art in me, and I in thee, that they also may be made perfect in one..." (John 17:21–23). So, it was taught in the Hindu Vedas; so it was taught in the Jewish Kabbalah; so it was written by the great Sufi mystic poets;

and so it was taught in all the great religious traditions of all time.

This "oneness" is our noble heart, which we share in the form of the inner peace I experience. Here, there is no differentiation between *you* and *me*. Both you and I are the same as the oxygen in the air! Set aside discrimination and bring awareness to your noble heart; you will constantly dwell in the reservoir of inner peace beyond your self-image and experience true happiness.

We will go through that process in the following chapters, starting from the alertness we are born with. When we improve our receptivity to alertness, we develop persistent awareness to engage with our noble heart and distance ourselves from our self-image—the mind. With that, we dwell in inner peace, where we can use our mind as a tool to be happy rather than be a victim of it.

As Socrates, who lived from 470 to 399 BCE, said, "The unexamined life is not worth living." We need to examine our life by exploring within to find our true selves. I know that you and I have different physical and mental self-images, but I recognize that it is not the case for our inner selves; they are the same. We need to explore within to recognize the oneness in each other.

Aristotle, a Greek philosopher who lived from 384 to 322 BCE, is considered one of the founders of Western philosophy. When he turned seventeen, he joined Plato's Academy in Athens and stayed until he was thirty-seven. Plato himself was a student of Socrates. Aristotle's writings cover various subjects, including physics, metaphysics, poetry, theater, music, logic, politics, ethics, biology, and zoology. His famous quotes include, "Educating the mind without educating the heart is no education at all." This brings us to our discussion about the doubt and the firsthand experience we need to recognize our true nature. Aristotle states that knowledge gathered through thinking and logical arguments is less helpful without experiential knowing—*educating the heart*. In other words, the thoughts and perceptions that create our minds are just intellect, but our heartfelt experiences—*intelligence*—are necessary for true happiness. Therefore, I aim to help you experience your true self and happiness rather than provide information for your conceptual understanding of true happiness.

You will no longer be a fish swimming around the ocean looking for answers but one who experiences true happiness beyond logical and conceptual pursuit.

It's like the ancient Eastern analogy of the frog's life. We live in the mind as a tadpole lives in water, and we run around without knowing that there is true happiness—dry land—beyond our mind-created self-image—*water*. Like the tadpole cannot comprehend dry land, our mind can't comprehend true happiness. But when a tadpole is transformed into a frog, it knows water is a separate medium that can be used for its benefits. So many inventors, creators, great philosophers, and sages gain this transformation to live blissfully and use their minds to help others effectively.

Many prominent personalities I am discussing here have expressed their discoveries and transcendence at young ages. So, you can do the same with the experiences you gain from the practices in this book. You will dwell in your noble heart and use your mind to live blissfully. In other words, you will live in your true self while using your fictional character for your and others' benefit. I sincerely wish to help you with transcendence by using the practices I am introducing throughout this book.

I welcome you to this expedition, where you can engage your true self to deal with life challenges while experiencing the bliss of being alive—*true happiness*.

Part I

Am I a Fictional Character?

True Story

When we read a novel, we learn about fictional characters created by the author. When I look back on my life story, I realize that my character is a fiction created by many others, and I am not that person at my core. I have been given a name created by my parents or someone close to them. I didn't know that until I realized I should not be pointing to my body and calling myself a baby or claiming a toy as a baby's toy. Later, it became my body and my toy when I realized I had been given an identity. Then I realized I had been given a name, without my consent, by which everybody could identify me. But I knew that it wasn't me, as you may know, in your essence, that you are not the person others think you are by your name or otherwise. So, this is not only my, but our, true story.

I was born in a rural village in Sri Lanka and grew up in a traditional Buddhist community. However, my parents never forced me to believe anything or pushed me to be a rich and famous adult, which was the common family ideal of the village. I was free to hang around with anyone I liked and do whatever I wanted. It may be that my parents saw something in me and didn't fear my getting into trouble, or perhaps they had many other things to worry about. Whatever the reason, it benefited me to become a constant explorer and experience true happiness.

With that opportunity, I associated with many people of different ages, creeds, religions, and nationalities. I treated them equally, irrespective of their attitudes toward me, and my open-minded approach and unwavering friendliness won their hearts. That allowed me to explore freely many community values and views and learn from them.

At school, I studied Liberal Arts subjects, but I was curious about my friends who studied science to become rich and famous members of society when they would grow up. Out of curiosity, I studied those subjects and did the experiments on my own at home. They told me that they dissected frogs at school, as part of biology studies, which I tried on my little play operating table at home. You may have done similar experiments or tryouts at one stage of your life, not particularly dissecting a frog but other things.

I used to have a playhouse lab in our garden shed, with bottles full of colored water. In my imaginary world, I was a scientist and an innovator. My brother and I built a wireless radio from scratch, following an instruction book published in the native—*Sinhala*—language. It was not quite an invention but a great exploration and achievement for us.

In my inner explorations, I discovered that the country's traditional Buddhist rituals are not exactly aligned with the Buddha's core teaching. I started to explore deeper by reading scriptures and trying to make sense of them by experimenting with them within me. I am sure you may have tried similar things or had doubts about your faith at that age. However, I could easily harmonize the critical arguments and logic of the scholars and religious activists, yet I was not convinced. My inner essence told me that discovery needs to be done within, rather than believing everything in the books.

According to the tradition in Sri Lanka, my name was registered with the village name of our ancestors, first, then the family's name, and at last, my given name, which is very different from the Western format of a person's name. When asked to establish my identity in their recording format, I had challenges convincing officials in other countries about my given name. My fictional character name created in Sri Lanka was not accepted elsewhere; I wish I could have had the opportunity to identify with my true self rather than by a given name!

You may have had a similar, more personal, or emotional identity crisis. You may have overcome that with some help from others or by looking inwardly. You may have come out of that crisis completely or suppressed it temporarily. I discovered that we can completely uproot those crises and experience true happiness, anytime, with pure skillful attention.

In my case, I have reformatted, shortened, edited, and used my name as it fits, like editing a book and its fictional characters. I respond to any name anyone calls me at their will, without any emotional impact, because I know that my true self is not that identity. I am sure, at a deeper level, you know that you are not the person others identify by your name. Once you interact with them for a while, you may realize that others are not as you had originally thought. So, what we see as a person's true character changes regularly. Especially regarding your close friends, siblings, or partners, whom you thought you knew very well, and who may sometimes change instantly. Not only that, but your self-image also changes from moment to moment when responding to different situations. So, aren't we living with fictional characters? I hope you will agree that our true self is something beyond those fictional characters!

We change because our concepts change, and our concepts change based on others' opinions and our speculations. I find that these concepts, thoughts and memories are part of our minds, and the mind is like a smartphone. We get information, opinion, logic, and process, store, and put the results onto the screen or into speakers. Likewise, our mind constantly collects data and re-creates our self-image; that is why I call it a fictional character. We can use it like we use our smartphones, if we know it is a tool and how to use it. First, we need to recognize that our mind is not our true self. It isn't easy to understand. Our true self is our pure attention or awareness that never changes. It is the same right now as when we were born. But you may not see that because your attention is buried in the maze of concepts in your mind.

I use a unique probe to demonstrate this in my group practices, especially when I have a younger crowd. It is a tall square-shaped bottle filled with slightly colored water and clear, pure coconut oil. Oil and water get mixed when the bottle is shaken, and you do not see anything other than colored water in that bottle. Then I set it aside on a table for them to observe the changes. After a couple of minutes, the water in the bottle separates from the oil, and the oil will float on the surface of the water, showing two different layers, oil and water, inside the bottle.

This demonstration shows what will happen if you settle down to calm your mind or pause your thoughts. Your attention is always lost in myriad thoughts and concepts like not seeing the oil in the shaken water bottle; you feel that your thoughts and concepts are your true self. If you stop following your thoughts and concepts, you can relax your mind and let your pure attention become prominent, like oil rising to the surface of water. Water is heavier than coconut oil, just as your thoughts and concepts can give you a headache, but pure attention or awareness brings true happiness.

I have been experiencing true happiness in my true self, and you may have had similar experiences at least once in your life. That is why you picked up this book and began reading. So do not doubt that your awareness is not your mind. When physically and mentally relaxing, you dwell in your pure awareness—attention. Pure attention means that you're alert, free from thoughts and perceptions.

Self-check

You can check this for yourself. When you are outside gazing at the sky, look through the clouds into the clear blue sky. After a few minutes, the clouds will clear away from your vision and you will connect with the deep sky above you. Let your essence connect with the clear sky. You will experience your pure attention. You will realize that thoughts, perceptions, and emotions are not yours; they are like clouds; they belong to your fictional character—*the mind*—and you are dwelling in your true self. Then, you have access to your true self—*inner peace*; you can enjoy the true happiness you were born with, your true self—*your true story*.

I have had this ability since childhood, which was confirmed later when I meditated and experienced the deepest inner peace. As a child, I saw everybody I met equally, and the social differences and discriminations were not conducive to me, and I am glad about it. When I relocated and lived in different countries and societies, such physical and social differences easily faded away within me. Apparent discrimination and divisions in different countries and communities didn't matter to me. Their reaction toward me differed from friendly to not so friendly. Instead of reacting to them, I responded equally and won their hearts. Hence, I experience my true self—*inner peace*—throughout my life. You, too, can experience true happiness if you disregard such differences and identities. I would like you to practice the following to experience the pleasantness coming through you when you are free from interference from discriminative thoughts, concepts, and perceptions. This pleasantness will later develop into inner peace and true happiness.

Practice # 01: Unleashing Identities
When you set aside all physical and social discrimination, you can experience your true self.

Please set aside all discriminatory identities that you may have about yourself and others. It may not be easy to do this completely with the deep-rooted concepts of your nationality, religion, and other differences. At least for a few minutes, close your eyes, clear all those thoughts, and pay attention to the silence and still nature within you. You will feel free from any of your self-identifications, such as your nationality, race, creed, or even your gender or sexuality. This will free your mind from limitations and bring pleasantness to your essence. This pleasantness is fundamental to finding your true self and inner peace. After a few minutes, you can open your eyes and contemplate the following.

The pleasant feeling you just had is the same as how you felt when you were a child, with no grasp of social and physical differences. As a child, you did not know discrimination. You were free of such concepts, and they were nothing to you, which allowed you to enjoy your life with pure attention. If you succeed in this, you will be released from the resistance—*friction*—that comes from all discriminatory perceptions. In this process, once you go beyond the identity of gender and sexual orientation as well, you break through your enslaved mind—*your fictional character*. You are free, and a sense of calm will rush through your mind and body. I trust that you can feel and recognize this phenomenon right now. Let go of all your identities and open your heart to sense peace within you. A sense of lightness and freedom from agitation will surge through your inner self. You have touched your true self, the noble heart, and inner peace to some degree.

Relax in this condition and dwell in the present as long as possible. It is a marvelous experience when you unleash the boundaries of identity perception and concepts created by others in your mind. This peaceful pleasantness is your first level of experience of intense bliss and your noble heart that will lead to true happiness.

Please stop reading and revisit the above practice if you can't feel that peacefulness right now. Please spend two minutes experiencing the pleasantness you get from this practice. This pleasantness is the freedom you experienced while being a toddler, without fear and doubt, making others love you without discrimination.

When I introduced this practice to a small group in Mesa, Arizona, one of the participants asked me, in a very friendly way and jokingly, "whether I should give up everything for this?" I replied in the same manner that you will experience supreme happiness with whatever you have. Once you experience true happiness, you will be content with what you have. I find that every bit of discrimination in us, which I like to call mental friction, brings misery and chaos. Our mind creates friction to protect our self-image. Many believe that this friction brings satisfaction, and they keep thinking it is their happiness. For example, one might think that being rich makes them happy and then discriminate against the poor. I have met many people who were extremely happy but not rich. Some discriminate against others with misinterpreted religious beliefs or to strengthen their group image. I will discuss this further in the upcoming chapters "Satisfaction" and "Happiness." We all have to let go of petty differences at the end of our life. So why not do it now and be free from them to experience true happiness throughout the rest of our lives?

Many great philosophers experienced true happiness and expressed it through philosophical theories, teachings, and quotes. I trust they did so because others who could deeply contemplate or experiment with those theories could also experience true happiness.

A good example is the cogito of René Descartes, who lived from 1596 to 1650. This quote in Latin, *"Dubito; ergo cogito. Ergo sum,"* that is, "I doubt; therefore, I think. Therefore I am," if you deeply contemplate on this statement, it means that we doubt our true selves; therefore, we think and act according to our minds' speculations, which create our self-images and their consequences. We will experiment with this, here, throughout this journey.

You've had a glimpse of a peaceful experience by letting go of discriminatory identities, perceptions, and mental friction.

Those identities are the fictional characters we portray to others, and when we let go of those, we become our true selves. It is as if we were on a stage, playing a role in a drama, and when the play is over, we let go of the character we were playing to return to our true selves. As long as we center ourselves with "I am," our fictional character exists, and once we let go of it, we see our true selves.

That will be the story of your true self, too. To help you on your way, I have refrained from mentioning gender, race, or color because doing so might unintentionally lead you to a biased expression or discriminatory perception. This includes what you think of me. As mentioned earlier, consider me one of your dear friends. I encourage you to keep an open mind to all possibilities, regardless of the characteristics that define our exteriors—such as male or female; child or adult; rich or poor; Black or white; able, differently abled, or challenged; and everything in between. When we let go of those, we become peaceful and more alive, and I hope you felt that, at least for a few moments.

Experiencing this feeling is helpful in highlighting that you were like a fictional character when you identified with those petty differences. Those identities are conceptual norms, neither real nor equal as, say, the color of our blood or the true self you experienced just a few minutes ago. When we set aside our differences, we experience true happiness at the surface level, with pure attention; later we can deepen it to inner peace.

Does your closest friend or partner know the real you—*your true self*, or do they know only your fictional character? Until now, you identified your "self" with your fictional character, but now you are beginning to feel your true nature. I do not doubt that you are a great explorer, and soon you will experience your true self and share that experience with many others, including those who are yet to be born into this world. We will explore more of this in the next few chapters, to discover who you are and your fictional character.

Explorer

Since birth, we have been exploring everything around us. That was always my longing, and I trust it is yours, too. This expedition to satisfy curiosity began from the inception of humankind, individually and collectively. We collectively explore nature, cities, countries, continents, the globe, and now the universe. We share the knowledge we acquire among ourselves, wishing good for humankind. Those explorations and discoveries are used for our benefit or detriment, like the discovery of atomic power used to produce electricity or kill on a mass scale. Individually, we explore things and activities around us, create our own world with myriad thoughts, perceptions, interpretations, and beliefs, simultaneously building our fictional characters. In this process of exploring, we inadvertently create our self-images, or egos. Some use their egos for high achievements; others get lost in their self-images and become victims of the mind. When we become victims of our minds, we rarely examine inwardly or explore within to recognize our true selves. Instead, we live in chaos and misery, searching for happiness.

As mentioned earlier, I have been an explorer since my childhood. I remember looking at every creature crawling on the earth, and later scanning through the bushes and trees in the wood. After I could ride a bike, I started to explore the nearby hills, streams, and other interesting places with my friends. When I look back, that exploration extended in two directions, external and internal. While I continue to travel and explore many countries and cultures outwardly, I did explore inwardly from my childhood. Here I am sharing my insight from my inward explorations, hoping to help you experience true happiness.

Self-check

As an explorer, you may have climbed mountains, traveled to many countries, and studied the globe and universe with much thrill and enthusiasm. This longing comes with a curiosity to know more about everything. We study and educate ourselves to discover and understand our conceptual world. However, exploring within and discovering our essence is rarely even attempted. Here, you are embarking on such an inner journey. Our emotions, desires, and fears are the valleys and mountains of the inner-self's landscape, and this exploration we undertake is to discover them within and understand our true selves. Pause for a moment and check to find out whether you know your true self or are still seeking it.

As children, we repeatedly ask "Why?" following every answer we receive from our parents until they give up answering. We continue that quest even as adults, looking for answers externally without exploring our inner landscape. This outer quest leads to confusion, chaos, and conflicts with others, and we need to recognize that questioning is not always helpful. Many get lost in those quests and strengthen their self-images — egos — making their own and others' lives miserable. Can you relate to this unfortunate situation we all can face?

From my experience, I found that our questioning fades away only when we recognize that the entire world is the concept we created within us. When we realize that seeking satisfaction from the outside is an endless exercise, we turn inward to explore. When we continue exploring within, we can experience inner peace: our true self. Then we see things differently. We recognize that the world we knew was just many accumulated concepts. You may already know this or maybe you are just beginning to discover it.

I saw that many people have examined their self-landscape with much enthusiasm and realized the true nature of life. They did it with great enthusiasm and an open mind. Only a few of them have shared that experience with others. I invite you to examine yourself with the same enthusiasm and excitement; it will benefit you and the people around you!

I find that exploring within is very rewarding, and I see that while our true self or noble heart is unique to us, it is present in every living being in the form of inner peace. It is interesting how we share inner peace with all humans and everything else on Earth and beyond. Individually, we experience it as our own true selves or noble hearts, but collectively it is the ocean of inner peace. As you read, draw your inferences without prejudice and try to absorb what is presented free of prior concepts. Pure attention is fundamental to this expedition of self-discovery.

Hopefully, as you experienced, once you release all identities, a sense of pleasantness and clarity of attention will surge through you. That is the preparation you need to access the noble nature of your heart and inner peace.

Self-check

As a self-check, consider your response to what you do for a living. You may either have a passion for your job or hate it. Your heart compels you to reflect on this issue, feel deeply about it, eventually guiding you to act to free yourself from this agony. However, while your heart offers such guidance, your mind pores over the implications of external events and reacts based on perceptions, beliefs, fear, and doubt. We get lost in the concepts, like oil mixed with water that cannot be seen. The heart always guides us to be in peace. The mind blocks and obscures your heartfelt intention with myriad thoughts, perceptions, beliefs, and fear of others' opinions of you. Since we distrust our intuition and the noble nature of the heart, we live in distress and fear. Unintentionally, we distract our need for well-being and go with confusing thoughts and speculations created by our enslaved minds. You might think you need to work and have no choice. Your mind cannot see any other option but to stick with your job while hating it. This is your fictional character trying to control and direct you through this miserable situation. I have been in this situation many times in my life. I dealt with it by trusting my intuition and inner peace.

The more you understand how your heart responds to life's situations, the more you will be inclined to trust it. You might not have the choice or option to change your job, yet you might have the choice or option to respond to this situation differently, without being a victim of the mind. You can explore within to see what makes you hate your job and then correct the cause. You may not like your boss's attitude, which causes you friction, or you may think others are doing a better job and fixate on that idea, clinging to it. When you eliminate such friction and clinging, you will be free from the concept of hate in your mind and start to love your job.

In the coming chapters, you will learn a few techniques to eliminate your friction and clinging by following your noble heart—*your true self*. These techniques will give you the confidence to draw on your inner peace and be happy in any stressful situation. I find it immensely interesting that the greater our experience of the heart's nobility, the better off we will be in all aspects. You will find yourself enriched in terms of your health, wealth, and stability, influencing your attitude toward the world at large. If you do not examine the depths of your heart with pure attention, you cannot draw on inner peace. When you cannot draw on inner peace, you are bound to suffer from stress, problems, confusion, and disarray. When I realized this, I became even more encouraged to explore within. I hope you, too, are eager to experience this phenomenon of true happiness.

You may assume that many things happening in the world are wrong and that you alone have the solutions to make this world a perfect place to live in. It might not occur to you that while your solution may temporarily satisfy your perception, the reality might be quite different for the rest of the world. This is because your mind deceives you into believing that only your solution will work and that it will benefit you. So, you continue the quest to satisfy that idea, which has no end. With this approach, you will not find the answers unless you keep an open mind to all possibilities.

I found that great self-explorers discovered this truth in a unique way and decided to correct their flaws. They saw the reality within themselves instead of correcting what they perceived as flaws in others. Devote more time to changing yourself rather than putting effort toward changing others. Criticizing others will not make you right, and it would be best if you explore yourself from within. Do not look for others' faults; look for your own.

Do not fixate on one view, be open to all possibilities, including what you are experiencing right now reading this book. You will see the benefits to yourself and others as changes take place within you. I am sharing with you the same experience I had. Please try the following practice to experience your friction-free true self.

Practice # 02: Realizing Your Self-Image
Identifying your self-image is more beneficial to you than changing others.

Close your eyes, relax, and spend some time experiencing the peace within you when you eliminate all identities, as you did in the earlier practice. You will feel pleasantness surging through your heart. It is similar to allowing a shaken bottle to settle on a table and watching the coconut oil rise to the surface of the water effortlessly.

Open your mind to all possibilities, including that it is not always the world that needs to change. Contemplate one thing you think should be changed in this world, and consider how many would appreciate such change. Settle in that notion and focus on the opposition to the change you would like to implement. This change doesn't necessarily need to be large-scale; it can be as simple and minute as confusing thoughts about your neighbor. You need to pay attention to the space between such thoughts. It is like looking through the clouds to see the clear blue sky. Then, that space will gradually open up, and a sense of peace will surge. You will feel pleasantness and calmness sprouting in you. This will give you pure attention to your true self. Then you will realize that you were living in a self-image with confusing thoughts, trying to change others to protect your fictional character.

Give yourself time to clear your mind in this condition and dwell in the present for as long as possible. You have released a layer of your self-image tainted with perceptions and concepts created by others about you. This pleasantness is another level of experience of intense bliss, and your noble heart will drive you to true happiness.

Please stop reading and revisit the above practice if you can't feel that peacefulness right now. Please spend two minutes contemplating and experiencing the pleasantness you get from this practice.

You may have heard those famous explorers confess that when they are climbing the mountain or at the peak of their expedition, they feel intense liveliness and pure attention to their surroundings. They see everything around them with amazing clarity, with no thoughts or concepts disturbing them at that time. They experience true happiness, and this bliss of being alive, this experience, encourages them to repeat similar, extremely dangerous expeditions. When they climb mountains as a group, they never blame or find fault with others. Because through their experience of true happiness — inner peace — they recognize that they are as one — oneness. Their bond is not just like close friends but a much deeper connection with inner peace. They see each other as one person who has a different self-image, but, on a deeper level, their true story is the same. This oneness is what we need to understand and experience. So do not look for others' faults. If you find faults in others, you are suffering from negative thoughts and speculations. Keep your mind free from unnecessary clinging and friction. That's the spirit of the inner explorer, too. You will sustain pure attention to experience true happiness, if you can do that.

Do you agree with the above analysis or think that those explorers are taking unnecessary risks? I find that those two lines of thought come from our inner characters. Though we all are explorers, we see things differently depending on the philosopher or sage in us. Similarly, we take different approaches when searching for happiness. You may not have labeled yourself as either, but there is a philosopher or a sage in you. Most of us have the qualities of a philosopher, and you become a philosopher or a sage depending on the extent you know your heart.

If you are a philosopher, you question most situations, searching for the best answer based on your intellect. This approach ensures that the answer is logical, coming from your mind rather than your heart. If you are a sage, you first experience the peace within and then relate to the external conditions to reflect on their significance. Many of us have varying degrees of qualities of both the philosopher and the sage.

According to historians, the ancient Greeks always viewed a philosopher as an eternal seeker of wisdom: someone who always searches for the truth and comes close to it but ultimately cannot attain perfect wisdom. Unlike a philosopher, the sage, in ancient Greece, was considered the bearer of wisdom — *one who already possesses wisdom and only needs to self-actualize.*

Whether you are a philosopher or a sage depends on the degree of your innate wisdom, which I would call true self — *inner peace.* The wisdom or inner peace you bear is always within you, no matter who you are. I find that irrespective of your approach, as a sage or philosopher, you can become a bearer of wisdom. In other words, you can dwell in inner peace using either of those approaches, and your wisdom flourishes. You will clearly recognize the reality of things happening inside and outside and become a bearer of wisdom.

I realized that understanding our inner character helps us to draw on our inner peace and be happy. In other words, our well-being is linked to the philosopher or sage within us. Once you recognize who you are, you can find your pathway to exploring your inner peace.

While on the subject, it is important to clarify that the heart and mind I am referring to are not the organs — *heart and brain* — within our bodies that keep us functioning physically. On the contrary, the heart is our alertness or our essence as human beings, and the mind is our thoughts, perceptions, and memories. There is no physical location or material substance in either of them. Our essence is our heart, which is always calm and peaceful and responds to situations without reacting emotionally. Our mind is full of thoughts that perceive the world, based on memories and judgments.

As you become more intuitive about your true self, you will access the peace within, and this process will help you understand how integral your noble heart is to your well-being.

I look to you, as an explorer engaged in this effort, to understand who you are and the noble nature of your heart, true self, and inner peace. Since I call you an explorer, your self-image has changed to an explorer. But it will change again to a philosopher or a sage in the next two chapters, where I discuss those characters in detail.

With your explorer hat on, we need to turn to explore inwardly, looking into your approach to life. We will use your skill in exploring outwardly to examine your true self inwardly.

The next two chapters are my attempt to help you understand to what degree you have the qualities of a philosopher or a sage. This may change your self-image from one to the other, and I will assist you in penetrating the philosopher or the sage in you. Through the insights thus gained, you will grasp the essential meaning of your life. Your curiosity to understand who you are will drive you to find your inner peace. As you continue to read, please critically examine and undertake the various self-checks and practices, like an explorer, to get a firsthand experience of your true self.

Philosopher

Most of us are philosophers and like to debate, argue, and logically consider what is right and what we think is wrong. Partaking in this activity, we strengthen our self-image as a philosopher. Though many of us may not identify as a philosopher, we do have the qualities of one. You started reading this book because you longed to find answers, which is a quality of the philosopher. Most of us take this approach and create a self-image apart from our true selves. Although we can use this self-image to interact with others, like a tool in our toolbox, our true self is not this. Some of us study one specific subject and strengthen our minds to use as a tool with which to make our living. Those who have done this may have been awarded credentials, and many are very humble about it. In this chapter, we will further explore whether a philosopher's approach is prominent in you, and, if so, how to explore your true self with that approach. You may have already settled on the idea that you are a philosopher, but if not, you can critically examine our discussion here and try the self-checks I have outlined to test and identify this character for yourself.

I personally associated with many philosophers, from my closest family members to prestigious doctorate holders from many colleges in different countries. I always understood their conviction, passion for the knowledge they gathered, and confidence in the logic and arguments. I respect and appreciate their skill in using the mind for goodness in the world. However, intuition sprouting from our true selves can create unthinkable wonders that we call inventions and innovations.

Such innovations are impossible with logical thinking because logic is based on preconceived concepts. Therefore, the self-image of a philosopher is also a fictional character.

Many of us are thinkers and philosophers. Conceptual theories and thinking dominate our minds. We try to resolve a problem with conventional norms. We question everything until a satisfactory answer is found. This is like children asking "Why?" for every answer from their parents. In this world, obtaining completely satisfying answers to any question is rare. As a result, many of us philosophers are driven to raise still more questions and get lost in the process. I have been in such situations, and I think it possible that you might have experienced similar positions at one time or another.

Those questions fade away only when we recognize that the whole world is within us and we create our world with our thoughts and perceptions. When I hear experts talking about the universe and galaxies from different dimensions, unique to their own understanding, I respond as if it were science fiction being created by those experts. They are conceptualizing some theory of how the galaxies came about.

Once we go deeper into our essence, we all are the same and can see how the galaxies in the universe came about without conceptualizing and formulating theories.

When philosophers contradict one another, they create new theories or new philosophies and never settle with others' opinions. I discovered that philosophers continuously seeking wisdom from the outside always end up with contradictions. They will rarely bear wisdom but will strengthen their self-images, their egos. I trust that you also have met some of them. Unfortunately, people can cling to logic or concepts that prevent them from seeing anything beyond. Like a tadpole swimming in the water, looking for dry land inside the water.

However, I find that great philosophers can go beyond their logic and self-images to become bearers of wisdom and great sages.

One example is Socrates, a great ancient philosopher from 470 to 399 BCE. He said, "People confer internal success upon themselves." He further wrote, "The secret of happiness, you see, is not found in seeking more, but in developing the capacity to enjoy less." In my assessment, the internal success he refers to is our inner peace, true self, or true happiness. In fact, Socrates was later recognized as a great sage in the Mosaic of the Seven Sages, now in the National Museum of Beirut, a work excavated from a Roman villa in Baalbek. This is believed to have been created in the third century BCE. This recognition proves that, eventually, a philosopher will become a great sage.

Like Socrates, many great philosophers gave up logical thinking and searched inwardly to discover the true meaning to their lives. I came to this conclusion because many of the philosophers I reference in this book speak to the same experience I had firsthand.

In my assessment, René Descartes, the famous French philosopher, mathematician and scientist, whom I referred to earlier, was one such individual. He is known as the father of modern Western philosophy, and much of the subsequent Western philosophy responds to his writings.

Descartes refused to accept the authority of previous philosophers because he recognized his true self apart from his mind. You can be like him, so do not believe in others' ideas. Descartes frequently set his views apart from those of his predecessors. Perhaps, at one stage, he changed his approach from seeking externally to exploring within. With that transformation into a great sage, Descartes expressed his best-known statement, "I think. Therefore, I am," as discussed earlier. I concluded that he was a great philosopher who eventually dwelled in inner peace—a bearer of wisdom or a great sage. He recognized the difference between living with a self-image created by the mind and having a blissful life with inner peace—the true self.

Descartes's statement directly points to our thinking, which creates our self-images. If you carefully examine it, you will see he directly addresses the self-image, or "I," which consists of our thoughts and perceptions—*our minds.* We need to apply our philosopher's approach as Descartes did and recognize the obstacles and resistance that hinder experiencing true happiness in our life. Great philosophers such as Descartes kept an open mind, challenged conceptual thinking, explored the intuition surging from their hearts, and realized that we are mind-created self-images. I hope you are with me on this. When Descartes said, "therefore I am," he directly addressed that thought makes our self-image.

On the other hand, controlled by our mind, we may be quite satisfied with what we do and enjoy seeking answers in our endless external quests. If so, we never realize that our cognitions are limited by our minds, darting around like fish in the ocean, looking for the so-called "ocean." So, you cannot experience your true self by thinking and conceptualizing.

In other words, we lose ourselves in a maze of questions, boost our self-images, dwell in a fictional character, and never accept the fact that our essence is peaceful and universal. We persistently challenge everything that comes from the inner essence in order to achieve some form of perceived satisfaction. In this pursuit, many people get confused and make their lives miserable. Also, you may have heard that some famous people go insane with their thinking and fall into unfortunate situations.

I noticed that pride in being a philosopher enhances one's ego or self-image, hindering the path to becoming a great philosopher. Great philosophers have always kept an open mind and explored the depths of their hearts.

Self-check

Let's say someone took the opportunity to stop a child from playing in the dirt, wishing for better hygiene. In comparison, the child becomes unhappy, while that person is happy. So, what is the correct answer in this situation? Is the person in the wrong by disturbing the child's happiness?

You might be glad to know that the child had fun with dirt and there was no friction. In that case, you are more of a sage than a philosopher, since you shared the child's joy. You had no problem with the child's action, and hopefully experienced the same joy or blissful sensation as the child. You are able to join with the child, and share in their joy and happiness.

I hope you can see your different inner characteristics by favoring one point of view; either the child's health or happiness is more important.

Likewise, we can get answers by exploring within. This means experiencing what is happening rather than having years of debates about it. In other words, knowing by experience rather than being satisfied with conceptualized beliefs.

My attempt here is to penetrate to the sage in you so that you can open your heart and distance yourself from your concepts to better recognize the philosopher in you. It is like you must come out to the dry land to see the water.

From ancient times, individuals have followed a path that has led them to recognize the heart's true nature and allowed them to dwell in inner peace. Consequently, they lived peaceful and blissful lives. I use the word *recognize* because our attention is what should dwell in inner peace. It is not an "understanding," which is always relative to what we think and conceptualize, the process that shapes a fictional character or self-image. "Understanding" is the making of the mind. When you recognize something with pure attention, you experience it firsthand in your cognitive field. If you are a philosopher, you need to shift your attention from conceptual thinking—*intellect*—to experiential knowledge—*intelligence*.

Many of us did not believe anything our parents tried to convince us of when we were children. We were curious and wanted to experience everything. As toddlers, we picked up things and tasted them to experience what they were, even dirt on the floor. Some of us refused to believe that fire will burn and hurt us until we put a finger into the flame of a candle. But, as we grew older, we started believing in others' opinions, so much so that we got emotionally attached to them and let them make our lives miserable. We cannot be happy if we get deeply attached or cling to others' opinions. As we did in childhood, we should recognize our true nature experientially.

We experientially learned a lot during our childhood that we cannot forget. If we were lucky, we enjoyed our life to the fullest while learning about ourselves and our surroundings until our elders planted the idea that we each need to become someone, that is, one who is respected by your society. This is how you start creating your fictional character. The opinions of others make us think fearfully about achieving such a mind-made goal, which gradually and surely takes away our happiness. This transformation is happening to children earlier than before in this information age. They talk and act like adults without enjoying their true selves in childhood, which passes by like the wind. We do not have to be victims of a fictional character created by others for us. We do not have to enact it.

It is not too late to regain the happiness you enjoyed in your childhood. You can embrace your childhood joyfulness and trace back to when you lost that blissfulness. It may have happened gradually, but it likely started with someone else's opinion, and your thoughts and perceptions wrapping around that opinion. Since then, you have identified yourself with it, pursuing fleeting satisfaction—*conceptual happiness*. You may be satisfied with something for a short time but look for greater satisfaction later, since your perceptions are renewing. You cannot go back to being a child, but that you can feel and live a child's life, and I trust that you can get such an experience by practicing the following.

Practice # 03: Feeling Like a Child
You cannot be a child again, but you can enjoy
a child's happiness.

Pause your reading and contemplate your childhood. Remember how much freedom you enjoyed during those days. You had no worries, commitments, or goals to achieve. You ran around, examined, and explored with an open mind to understand everything in and around you. You were free like a bird, flying from one tree branch to another. Birds do not have a goal to achieve except to be alive. Please feel that freedom. Notice the pleasantness emerging in you. You will feel relaxation running through your body and mind. Recognize inner peace and bliss emerging in you. I always experienced this when I took my attention to my worry-free childhood. I hope you got the same experience, freeing you from your philosophical and confusing thoughts. If not, try this practice again and enjoy inner peace, clear of any thoughts, by looking at a toddler or a picture of a toddler. This will bring humility to your philosopher qualities and open your heart, allowing you to see the fictional character in yourself.

This condition of humility will clear your mind to dwell in the present moment. You have released another layer of your self-image, tainted with perceptions and concepts created by others. Before those concepts were planted in you, the child's happiness existed in your true self, and once you experience this, you will see your blissful noble heart.

Suppose you can't feel that happiness right now? Then please stop reading and revisit the above practice. Please spend a few minutes experiencing the joy and happiness you had when you were a child.

The experience you had with the above practice will give you access to your inner peace to some extent. Based on that foundation, you can see the philosopher in you working fearlessly to obscure true happiness. Therefore, this philosopher is another self-image you may cherish without knowing it, which is blocking your inner peace.

We humans are one species with equal capabilities, irrespective of the petty differences we conceptually cling to. As a result, many of us philosophers are driven to seek satisfaction created through our concepts. Once we were children full of joy and happiness, but as we got older, that happiness evaded us and was replaced with perceptions collected from books and others' opinions. Seeking satisfaction dominates in many philosophers' minds.

William James, who lived from 1842 to 1910, was a leading thinker of the late nineteenth century, one of the most influential philosophers, known as the "Father of American Psychology." He was the first educator to offer a psychology course in the

United States. His famous quote, "There is only one thing a philosopher can be relied upon to do, and that is to contradict other philosophers," sums up the approach of many of us and is also the definition of a philosopher given in ancient Greek civilization. I found that when we take this approach, we will not find lasting happiness but fleeting satisfaction. Unless you have an open mind, it isn't easy to see an end to this quest. Instead of following this method, you can sensibly analyze life situations and respond to them with your heartfelt intuition. If you do so, you will recognize the noble nature of your heart and live a happy life, dwelling in your true self. I trust that the sages have had this inclination from birth, and philosophers need to find it.

You may be a philosopher looking for logical answers to your quest. As mentioned earlier, there is a sage in you as well. The next chapter will discuss to what extent you have the qualities of a sage and how to use them to identify your self-image.

Sage

As we discussed earlier, you may have already recognized the sage in you by responding with compassion to the child who plays in the dirt. You saw the child in you, did not react to the situation, and feel that the child was having fun in the dirt and responded to that. If philosophical arguments and conceptual theories are not for you, and you know there is a reason for everything, then you are in the category of "sage." At the same time, you may have the qualities of a philosopher to a lesser degree. That is why you are reading this book. I, myself, had been shifting from philosopher to sage until the day I experienced true happiness on a deeper level, in 1996. With that experience, I realized I had always been a sage, but my mind did not allow me to enjoy true happiness. This is a good moment for you to look back on your life and see whether you have had the qualities of a sage surface from time to time, but your mind mistakenly took them for short-lived satisfaction.

The Buddha was one of the great sages who lived around 500 BCE. Even today, his insight influences many people to recognize true happiness and live peacefully. Many scholars categorize the Buddha as a philosopher and consider his teachings a philosophy rather than a path or way of life. When you examine his biography, he had every external indulgence as a prince from birth but was driven to seek answers within. He then encountered the reality of life and realized that seeking within is the only path to liberate oneself from the enslaved mind — *the fictional character*. Thus, Buddha began his teaching, a path to overcome the enslaved mind, based on the firsthand experience he gained through his practice — *after awakening* — rather than on conceptualized philosophy. His teaching is to recognize and be aware that "the mind is the forerunner of life," and to awaken to a blissful life free from the sufferings created by our mind. That should be our goal. The word awakening or *nirvana* means blowing out the self-image or "quenching" the activities of the worldly mind and its related consequences—suffering.

In my assessment, Eckhart Tolle, born in 1948, the author of the best-selling book *The Power of Now,* is one of the greatest sages in this modern era who lives in his true self. He teaches us to be in the present, free from the mind-made frictional self, with its heaviness and its problems, in other words, free from living in the unsatisfying past and the fearful future. He was a seeker who pursued his search by studying philosophy, psychology and literature. He graduated from the University of London and was a postgraduate researcher at Cambridge University. He stopped pursuing his doctorate after his sudden inner transformation at twenty-nine. He began to feel a strong underlying sense of peace in any situation, and he teaches with firsthand experience of what true inner peace is.

Tolle writes that "the most significant thing that can happen to a human being is the separation process of thinking and awareness," and that awareness is "the space in which thoughts exist."

This space is inner peace, the nobility of our heart, our true self.

A similar message is delivered in different forms by most common religions' teachings, such as be with God, be in the present, and find liberation or enlightenment. Therefore, you do not have to change your faith or the path you have already chosen to follow your own heart, dwell in inner peace, and live in your true self.

In appearance, most sages are virtuous, calm, and composed. You may have noticed a few of those types in your community, or you could be one of them. If you see things quite differently from others and always see that there is a reason for any situation and that it is to be accepted as it is, you are far from being a philosopher.

Let me elaborate further: You may tend to get carried away with the short-lived pleasures but occasionally recognize that such satisfaction does not have much worth. You are a sage who dislikes the self-image to a certain degree. In your heart, you know that something in you is pulling you into a territory you do not like. This pull is your thirst for satisfaction, denying your true happiness. Therefore, even if you have the qualities of a sage, your fictional character will continue to conjure a desire for fleeting satisfactions, believing it is better even though it brings unhappiness to your life. I am sure I do not have to give examples; you have your own experiences. Briefly, you may be satisfied; once it has ended, you will suffer and seek further satisfaction. You may accumulate vivid perceptions and memories of things and conditions around you, clinging to them inadvertently and falling into the mind's trap. Blinded by those traps, you speculate everything and seek fleeting satisfaction. By clinging to specific views, perceptions, and expectations, you strengthen your self-image and reject others and your own happiness. Hence your qualities of a sage may fade away. Be careful of mind traps!

Self-check

If you can see a reason for any and every situation, then short-lived pleasure is not for you, and you will likely prefer peace in others, nature, and yourself. You are far from a common philosopher, and that is because you see life sharply, like a sage. If your self-image were an onion, you would not peel it off layer by layer. Instead, you would want to cut it in half and investigate the onion inside out. Spend just a few moments and examine who you are and what approach you prefer, as it comes from your inner essence. Do not let your enslaved mind suppress your intuition. Draw your attention to the inner essence and connect with your inner peace. Peace is the pleasantness you feel, free of agitation and tension in the body and mind. When you have pure attention, this smooth sensation will surge and spread in you and into your surroundings. In other words, you are experiencing blissfulness, the noble nature of your heart.

When this bliss is sustained to a higher degree, we refer to it as inner peace—true happiness. The sense of peace within you is attributable to your openness and receptivity to bliss—the noble heart. You cannot conceptualize and interpret bliss; you need to experience it firsthand. Great sages can do this instantly under any circumstances. You could also become one of them by accessing the experiences from the practices outlined in this book.

In any happy moment, you will feel blissfulness. When bliss appears, pay attention and sustain it for as long as you can. If you succeed, there is no room for the enslaved mind to interfere with your true happiness. That is the true self you came into this world as, and have been from birth and are now.

In contrast, the unexamined mind always seeks fulfillment in perceived happiness and satisfaction, like a tadpole swimming around and looking for water. Philosophers are constantly in this rat race. If you are a sage, your mind may occasionally carry you away with myriad thoughts and interrupt your happiness. However, if you are a great sage, you will simply recognize this and bring your attention back to inner peace, just as a frog can jump out from the water to dry land at any time.

Perhaps, up until now, you neither noticed nor recognized it as an expression of the nobility of your heart. If you recognize pleasantness in you and allow it to flourish, your blissful experience will last. If you recognize bliss frequently in your life, you should consider yourself a sage.

As the Buddha said, the human mind — created with thoughts and perceptions — is a powerful faculty and the forerunner of life. It can distract even certain sages' inner peace, turning a person into a monster and making them suffer from delusions. If you think of yourself as a sage simply because you have cherished that image in your mind and cling to it, you may be more of a thinker than one who bears wisdom and dwells in inner peace. It may not be apparent or recognized until you try a few self-checks to explore within.

Once I faced a situation with one of my superiors, who had the reputation of getting things done by dominating and pressuring others. We had a long discussion on one subject, and I could see all the noise was just an ego-building exercise to establish authority as a new superior. As usual, I responded to all the questions without any emotional display, and I was not surprised to hear the final question: "Don't you have an ego?" Then I realized that person's effort was to use my emotion to get the work done.

You may have come across many similar situations on your life journey. In such situations, I can be as calm as undisturbed water and free from any disturbing thoughts. You could do the same.

Focus on a mirrorlike lake that has a clear and calm surface. It would help if you cleared all mind-created distractions, thoughts, perceptions, memories and emotions to be like that lake. This will open your heart to see the world as it is, just as you can see the undistorted reflection of the surroundings and sky on the still waters. You will dwell in inner peace. From that base, you can respond to any situation without getting agitated.

The water's clarity and stillness emphasize the sharpness and accuracy of your mind. You will be able to experience the world's reality as it is, undistorted by your mind's distractions. This is also like noticing the birds chirp through the silence of the dawn. As a sage or a philosopher, your goal would be to achieve clarity of heart and allow peace within to reign and usher in blissful living.

Although you may be unaware of it, recognizing the bliss within your noble heart brings true happiness. This is the underlying reward that you have been seeking all along. You can be free from your mind, whether you are a philosopher or a sage. Then you will enjoy your life rather than hate it and experience true happiness inwardly and outwardly.

Next, with your sage's approach, we will examine whether you are a sage or pretending. Your mind may project a persona of a sage while you are still clinging to your self-image. With the following practice, you can let go of the self-image of the sage in you and become a true sage.

Practice # 04: Releasing Clinging
Emotional clinging creates our self-image.

Before starting this practice, you need to try the previous practices at least once to get a sense of your pure attention, free from any discrimination and friction, to penetrate the sage in you. With that, you get a certain experience of keeping pure attention for at least a few minutes. You commence this practice with the following steps.

Please take a deep breath and hold it for as long as possible. When it becomes unbearable, release it while relaxing your body. You will feel the release of tightness in your body and mind and a higher degree of relaxation. Stay with that relaxation and examine yourself at the deepest level to see whether you find any tightness left in the body. Also, check whether you still feel frustration and unhappiness in your mind. Try this a couple of times to settle yourself into deeper relaxation.

You feel relaxed because you let go of clinging to your body and mind. We hold both our body and self-image tightly and cling to them. This clinging is the fundamental cause of suffering when emotionally attached to anything. You do not have to reject or accept anything. Be neutral about them to be happy.

The neutral feeling will clear your mind to dwell in the present to a certain degree. You have peeled another layer of your self-image that clings to your body and mind perceptions and to concepts created by others. Once you release the tightness of your body, which is caused by your holding on to your emotional attachment, you feel a sense of freedom leading to true happiness.

Suppose you can't feel that happiness right now? Please stop reading and revisit the practice. Please experience the relaxation of body and mind that comes from this practice. As previous practices helped you to achieve this, you can appreciate this experience while trying the rest of the practices introduced in upcoming chapters.

If you recognize the ease of your body and mind, you are more of a sage, and you need to be honest and respond to your intuition without doubt and fear. This is the key to opening your heart, free from clinging and friction. Then you will respond to any distress that comes to you like a mirror image of nature reflecting on still water, without making any ripples. There won't be any impact on your inner peace, and it will not be distressing, but perhaps a confirmation and welcome reminder of the fictional character.

Before you turn to the next part of the book, I want to emphasize the fundamental aspect of our expedition. The philosophical and logical arguments are based on our fleeting thoughts and perceptions. They may satisfy us briefly but will never make us happy. However, our firsthand experiences will never fade. When we experience inner peace, we recognize the nobility of our heart to sustain true happiness and well-being.

I trust that the self-checks we have done so far have helped you to recognize your approach to life. Since we established our base as a philosopher or a sage, we can further explore our true selves. Please examine yourself and settle on one or the other, although you may have some qualities of the one you don't choose to a lesser extent. Either way, I trust that you realize we live with a fictional character. It is like a salmon seeing dry land on the bank of the river while leaping from the water on their way upstream to lay eggs. Likewise, you get a glimpse of your true self by unleashing your identity, realizing what self-image is, and eliminating clinging to feeling like a child when you did the practices during this part of our journey.

Now you know your self-image is a fictional character of a philosopher, a sage, or one in between. This is irrespective of what you think you are like: a good man or woman, father or mother, spouse or friend, manager or worker, leader or follower, or anything you have created as your self-image. Therefore, in the next part of our journey, we need to explore our true selves further by answering the question: What is our true self?

Part II

What Is Our True Self?

Einstein

I find that Albert Einstein is an excellent role model of a prominent figure who lived a true self all his life. He provides proof to identify our true selves when we examine the fictional character he portrayed to others. I consider Albert Einstein one of the great sages who recognized and lived with his true self from birth. At age two, he had to create a fictional character to interact with others.

He lived from 1879 to 1955 and is known worldwide for his scientific discoveries and the hardship he endured during his life. Einstein shared a lot of wisdom and insight into life, people, and the world in general. He concluded that we would understand everything around and within us through nature by stating: "Look deep into nature, and then you will understand everything better."

Even though he was a philosopher of science, the above is one of his famous quotes. On a special note, Einstein's philosophical thinking was driven by the solution of problems first encountered in his work in experimental physics. He is known as a great physicist, with his hallmark theory of special relativity expressed in the 1905 equation $E=mc^2$.

I came across the simplest explanation for Einstein's equation given by Sadhguru—born in 1957—one of the great sages of the present time. As Sadhguru reveals in his book *Inner Engineering: A Yogi's Guide to Joy:* "When Einstein gives us the formula $E=mc^2$, he is, put simply, saying that everything in the universe can be seen as just one energy. Religions all over the world have been proclaiming the same thing using somewhat different terminology when they assert that, 'God is everywhere.'"

After studying his character, I recognize Albert Einstein as a born sage who lived in his noble heart and became one of the most famous scientific celebrities, beginning with the confirmation of his general relativity theory in 1919 by Arthur Eddington. Einstein was so well-known in America at that time that he would often be stopped by people on the street and asked to explain his theory. He told them, "Pardon me, sorry! Always I am mistaken for Professor Einstein."

This anecdote was published in *The New Yorker* column "The Talk of the Town" sometime before World War II.

You may think Einstein lied to avoid the questions or the situations. But I think he genuinely identified Professor Einstein as his fictional character, not his true self. He did not need to lie, but others may think otherwise.

My intuition tells me that Einstein studied mathematics to explain our true nature to others in a meaningful way that they can understand. Until the age of two, he did not utter a word. At eight, he began studying advanced primary and secondary school education. At twelve, Einstein taught himself algebra and geometry over a single summer. Soon, he would excel in mathematics at such a high level that his family tutor wouldn't be able to follow his work.

Walter Isaacson wrote in his book *Einstein: His Life and Universe* that "Einstein's passion for geometry and algebra led the 12-year-old to become convinced that nature could be understood as a 'mathematical structure.'"

In the same book, Walter Isaacson revealed that Einstein stated: "Imagination is more important than knowledge."

He also said, "There should be extensive discussion of personalities who benefited mankind through independence of character and judgment."

So, Einstein did see that the true personality—*self*—independent of the fictional character benefits humanity.

Our intuition or imagination is more important than knowledge gathered from outside, and that means we need to go beyond our self-image to be with our true selves to benefit all of us and live blissfully.

Einstein has been the subject of or inspiration for many novels, films, plays, and works of music. He is a favorite model for depictions of absent-minded professors. I agree with that judgment. He distanced his mind and lived in his noble heart, and all social or common conventions were irrelevant to his true blissful life. So people labeled him as an absent-minded professor.

He promoted experiential knowledge by stating that:

"I prefer an attitude of humility corresponding to the weakness of our intellectual understanding of nature and of our own being."

I can see that this preference comes from his true self with the experience of the bliss of being alive—*true happiness*. He saw the weakness in intellectual understanding to recognize the true nature of our life—*our own being*. We can only experience our true self and cannot understand it through concepts.

In addition, his views on religion, philosophy, and politics indicate that he tried to bridge the gap between science or philosophy and reality. He saw the same bridge explained by great sages and said in a letter dated September 1937 published in the book *Albert Einstein, the Human Side: Glimpse from His Archives*, edited by Helen Dukas and Benesh Hoffman: "What humanity owes to personalities like Buddha, Moses, and Jesus ranks for me higher than all the achievements of the enquiring and constructive mind."

With my firsthand experience, I can relate to the similarities between Einstein, the Buddha, Moses, Jesus, and the like. I see the reason behind Einstein expressing the above view. Einstein never criticized any spiritual teachers—personalities—but religions are created by followers who inevitably misinterpret their teachers' messages. Einstein praised the spiritual teachers but criticized the religions created after their passing. That is why he refers to the great teachers as personalities rather than talking about their teachings as religion. He ranked all such personalities higher than all the achievements of the mind's quest and discoveries.

Self-check

I will discuss these individual personalities and their message in the final part of "How to Experience Our True Selves?" In the meantime, clear your mind from any concept and prejudice about any religion, faith, or spiritual teaching. You'll note that the world's most renowned scientists, like Einstein, did not discriminate against any of those teachers. So, please let go of the concept of science as the only way we can understand things. Spiritual teachers are trying to provide the experience of that which you cannot comprehend with your mind, and I am here to help you build that same bridge to experience your true nature.

When I read through *Einstein: His Life and Universe*, I found that he attempted to theorize and explain different layers of our cognitive field as described in Eastern meditative absorptions. According to Isaacson, Einstein's third paper explained the jittery motion of microscopic particles in liquid. To me, that resembles the elements in matter formation of existence described in Eastern philosophies.

Einstein's fourth paper explains his General Theory of Relativity. Then, in the fifth paper, he expanded the Special Theory of Relativity to establish the relationship between energy, mass, and speed of light to produce the best-known equation of all physics, E=mc². As I mentioned earlier, this theory is not different from the core message of original teachers of prominent religions who talk about oneness or emptiness.

When closely examining the "causal effects" described in Buddha's teaching, existence occurs depending on the related cause. Buddha named this "Dependent Origination"—*Patichcha Samuppadha.*

Advanta, Vedanta—*Vedic Scripture*—explains non-duality beyond the dualistic existence explained by Einstein's theory. As I mentioned earlier, Sadhguru sees the same similarity. Einstein was able to formulate his theory because he dwelt in the realm beyond dualistic existence, and he lived in his true self, not in self-image. It's like only a frog can explain the qualities of water since it is sitting on dry land, but a tadpole can't because of its never being on dry land.

All these similarities and comparisons can be accepted only with a deeper experience of your true self. Therefore, some of the points I am revealing here may not be conducive to your mind. But you will recognize them through your pure attention once you experience inner peace. I trust the practices I introduce in this book will help you experience this phenomenon.

As Eckhart Tolle aptly said, "The secret to finding the deeper level in the other is finding the deeper level in yourself; without finding it in yourself, you cannot see it in the other." The deeper level you see in others is the non-dualistic and neutral inner peace you share with them. When you see the universal nature of your noble heart, your compassion, empathy, and love for yourself and others will become inevitable and equal. You will easily recognize their points of view, the deeper meaning, and their origin.

Einstein discarded Newton's theory by being in the true self since he clearly saw that there is no absolute space and time in this world; they are only flickering matters falsely displayed as absolute by the speed of light. This reality can be experienced only through deep meditational absorption.

Walter Isaacson revealed this in *Einstein: His Life and Universe,* stating:

"Based purely on thought experiments—performed in his head rather than in a lab—Einstein had decided to discard Newton's absolute space and time concept."

Most of Einstein's theories are not yet proven in a lab but by mathematics. We use our minds like we use a smartphone as a tool and settle on the answers in mathematical equations because that is the only way a fictional character can comprehend them. When you experiment in your head, you do it by dwelling in your true self, inner peace. If the head—mind—is your lab, the person who performs experiments is your pure attention, which is not mixed up with your thoughts. This true self can be recognized through advanced meditation methods, which help us perceive the phenomenon beyond materiality.

In the same book, Isaacson stated: "There was a harmonious reality underlying the law of the universe, Einstein felt, and the goal of science was to discover it."

This harmonious reality is our true self, the inner peace we all share. We create our fictional characters on it. Our goal should be to find it, and Einstein expected science to discover it. However, the same discovery is done in the ancient and modern days by calming the mind and elevating pure attention.

Therefore, some of the points I expressed here may not be true for you until you see the deeper level of your true self. If you have not experienced it yet, I would like you to try the following practice to take you another step closer to it:

Practice # 05: Experiencing Silence
You can embrace inner peace by spreading your
attention to the silence in the dawn.

You have been elevating your pure attention, free of certain surface-level obstacles such as discriminative identities and clinging to ideas. You have touched the happiness you experienced as a toddler, too, and this practice will take you further into the silent nature of your heart to enable you to recognize your true self.

When you have free time, spread your attention to the silence in and around you, and embrace the freshness and calmness in the surroundings. It is more effective if you can do this at dawn. You can recognize the ease, pleasant conditions, and inner peace by embracing the surrounding freshness and calmness in the dawn. Dwell in it and pay attention to occasional disturbances such as a bird's chirp or the sound of passing vehicles. Then bring back your attention to the silence or space between those noises. Expand your attention into the silence between them until those noises fade away from you. This basic practice will elevate your inner silence. I often practice this, and the inner silence becomes so intense that I can hear my heartbeat in the midst of other noises.

You can do this when you wake up in the morning, while still in bed. Here, you may hear the ticking of the clock disturbing your silence. Move your attention to the space between two ticks and let your awareness blossom in that silence effortlessly. Eventually, the ticking sound will fade away, and you will be drawn into inner peace—*your true self.*

When your core is silent, perceptions and thoughts are like the birds' chirping in the silent dawn. You will clearly recognize that those thoughts are not part of you, just as you have recognized a bird's call or a clock ticking. Our thoughts and perceptions are like the surrounding noises;

when we pay attention to them, they become our thoughts. When you dwell in inner silence, you can clearly distance the noise — *thoughts* — from the calm and quiet surroundings. You can let go of them as you did with the birds' calls or the clock ticking by paying attention instead to inner peace. Try this practice for a few minutes and see how deep you can take your attention. The bliss in you will surge and flourish within your body and mind. You will experience happiness in the truest sense.

With such an experience, you will realize that Einstein's statement, "Look deep into nature, and then you will understand everything better," should not be taken lightly. It has a profound meaning, uttered from his own experience of inner peace, and we can examine this further by exploring the wonders of nature.

As children, we all learned a lot from nature. You may recall watching butterflies flying around and landing on beautiful flowers at will, with no particular order. You may have curiously observed a procession of ants marching on the path they themselves created. For many of us, nature was once our teacher; we experienced many miracles of nature, being there and marveling with no concern about time. Not all children are fortunate enough to have such a carefree childhood; you may not have had a chance to observe and enjoy such beauty and learn from nature in this information age. The new generation should be full of intelligence since they do not have to study and memorize a great many things because all the data is available at their fingertips. Therefore they can spend more time learning from nature, which needs to be done experientially. We can discuss and elevate such learning by looking deeply into nature. That is what we will do in the next couple of chapters.

Nature

As mentioned earlier, we were born with pure attention, our true selves. You see joy and happiness in a newborn's eyes. However, when we grow up, we lose that pure attention to the labyrinth of our minds. You may have noticed that when a plant is growing, it is alert to the light and warmth of the sun. Plants grow toward the sunlight. Some plants and trees are very alert throughout the day, tilted toward the sun; they wake up at dawn and go to sleep at dusk. From birth, the things around us are alert and awake in every moment and enjoy the liveliness and blissfulness in their surroundings except, perhaps, many of us humans, who are victims of our minds. Many of us do not find this blissfulness and liveliness within us or in nature. As Einstein said, we need to pay attention and look deeper to see the liveliness in a tree standing before us and its connection to us.

Self-check

At this point, many questions might likely arise in your mind. The initial ones would probably include, "What kind of an idea is this?" or "How can we be interconnected with nature?" You may be seeking answers to those questions just as philosophers do for every quest that comes to mind. Your desire to seek answers is an indication of the philosopher in you. This self-check is to see whether you are still taking a philosopher's approach. Many questions and issues are created in our minds, impacting only our fictional characters. When you live in your true self, you can see that every incident only impacts your self-image. If you cannot see that now, you will certainly find that as you explore within and recognize inner peace. With that, you will find the answers you may need for many other questions in your life.

In my life, nature is one of my teachers. Every morning I'd like to be outside and be with nature, embracing its calmness and freshness, giving me the touch of my true self to reflect on my fictional character. Then I see all issues, problems, mishaps, and pleasurable incidents happening to my fictional characters. None of them impact my true self, and they're happening at a distance within my self-image. I do not react to them but respond if I need to; otherwise, I'll be silent on them. Silence is a great tool for living life peacefully and blissfully. We experience silence in the dawn, which is also in us; similarly, our inner peace is in nature. To experience this, please try the following practice and dwell in inner peace in nature.

Practice # 06: Sharing Inner Peace
The majestic presence of trees offers you the
experience of inner peace that it shares with nature.

Do you consider a tree a living being? It stands tall like a giant, and its mighty structure is visible to all who gaze upon it. It is steady and filled with stillness and silence. With the arrival of autumn, it sheds its leaves and stays in a dormant state through winter. With the advent of spring, leaves and buds sprout on its branches, and summer sees them blossom. The tree grows leaves and flowers and bears fruit until the following autumn, like a human waking up in the morning to be active during the day and then retiring for the night to rest before the next day dawns. Compare a tree with a human by equating a year in human life to a day in a tree's life. In other words, the three hundred days within a tree's life span would translate into three hundred years in human life. Pause for a moment and fathom all that you just read.

Then imagine you are the giant tree that stands tall and still, with a life span of three hundred years. With that, sense the quietness and steadiness of the tree running through your whole body and mind. Your instinct will help you to experience this stillness and pleasantness. Pause a few moments to allow for that to happen in you. Then recognize the peacefulness emerging from your heart. This practice should bring a sense of calmness to you in your surroundings. Dwell in this calmness and experience the inner peace you share with the tree and nature.

Stop reading and do this practice a few more times to relax your body and mind. Your sharp alertness — pure attention — that you are born with will emerge within and flow into the nature of inner peace.

Your self-image may flatly deny this experience, or you may easily ignore a tree's connectedness to our existence. Perhaps you don't see a tree as anything more than a mere commodity for humans to utilize for comfort. A tree, you might contend, provides shade and fruit during the summer and firewood in winter. The solid branches merely represent another product that can be utilized to satisfy many needs. Humans have used trees, a readily available natural resource, in the past and will continue to do so in the future. Therefore, you have reason to deny that they are living beings and have any connection to your true self. These reasonings are coming from your philosopher's attitude; hopefully, you can see that they are no longer valid.

Self-check
Pay close attention to what your mind and heart have to say about these ideas. You may simply accept the notion of a tree as a living being or find yourself challenging its validity with

a series of questions. Whatever response you finally settle on will offer an interesting insight into the depths of your heart and, consequently, your approach to life as a philosopher or a sage. Your choice lays bare the true nature of your heart, which has often been misunderstood as the working of your mind.

It gives you a fascinating experience. I wonder if you have recognized the philosopher in you challenging the validity of the tree as a living being? If you did experience the inner peace that you share with a tree, or you saw that the life of a tree is similar to yours, then the qualities of a sage are surfacing in you.

Everything in nature is filled with bliss, the same energy we experience in our bodies. When you cut a tree branch, the same energy heals the scar, just as a cut in your skin heals, usually without any treatment. If you set aside all scientific explanations of how a wound gets healed without treatment, you will be able to recognize that the tree also shares the same energy as you do. Some call this an energy field, intelligence, and the liveliness that is common to every being on this planet. This energy generates such miracles as the healing of wounds and illness. I refer to our bliss as this energy field or the liveliness in nature. The bliss emerging from inner peace heals us and all living beings on this planet and beyond. We need to recognize this fact and allow such healing to occur without interruption from our enslaved minds. This bliss is the universal energy field summarized in Einstein's equation of $E=mc^2$, which I like to call inner peace.

We need to develop the habit of paying attention to this energy field that allows us to be happy without getting depressed, becoming insane, and being victims of our minds. This energy field is nature's freshness and liveliness, inner peace emerging everywhere and within us. Paying attention to liveliness in nature will enhance your inner peace, just as the day gradually gets brighter with the sunrise.

Whenever I enjoy the scenery or walk in the woods, I experience this inner peace within and without. We all do that in that kind of situation, but you may not recognize it as inner peace, though you may remember feeling relaxed and peaceful while walking in the park. The following practice will bring you a similar experience if you can relate to it.

Practice # 07: Embracing Nature

You can embrace the freshness in nature by spreading your attention beyond conventional boundaries.

By engaging with the previous practices your receptivity to the noble heart has improved. You can now experience your true self wherever you are. Here is a practice you can do while walking in the woods or park to help you recognize nature's energy of inner peace. Look at the trees and shrubs around you. They are fine as they are; there are tall, short, hollow, and all kinds of trees and shrubs. They are better off than most humans who live with anxiety, depression, and many other mental issues. They are not running around looking for happiness; they are happy being still and embracing the freshness and calmness in the air. Some yogic practitioners live their lives just like trees and shrubs, absorbing freshness and humidity in the air.

Please still your mind, and embrace the surrounding freshness during the walk by extending your attention beyond your body and other conventional boundaries. Spread your attention to the trees and shrubs before and behind you. You do not have to look around, just expand your attention to them and also to the space between them, in front and behind you. You should sense, at your deepest level, the joy and happiness that trees and shrubs enjoy by being still and sturdy. With your in-breath, you may bring that freshness and aliveness in nature into your body and mind. You may feel the joy and happiness filling your mind and body. With your out-breath, spread that experience throughout the space you share with the surrounding trees and shrubs.

Experiment with this practice a few times to see whether you can embrace the liveliness of nature at a deeper level. Make this a habit whenever you are out walking in the woods or in a park. It is one of my habits. Whenever I walk out in nature, I enjoy that stillness and pleasantness within me. I see the minute details of a tree, its branches, and the space between its leaves. I experience the stillness and pleasantness coming from them. Therefore, don't forget to repeat this practice while walking outside.

You may find the joy and happiness that stems from this practice are quite different from your preconceived notions of joy or happiness. This is the bliss you share with the trees, shrubs, and other living beings. Please do not mistake it for satisfaction, which formulates around the mind-created perceptions that we will discuss later in the next part of our journey.

Recently I tried to uproot a weed in my backyard, and I felt its liveliness and vibration running through its stem as soon as I touched it. It is like we feel blood running in our veins. My noble heart directed me not to proceed with my action. You can check this for yourself by touching any soft plant stem or herb growing in the earth, thriving with support from Mother Earth. Touch it with bare hands and pure attention, and you will sense the plant's liveliness and the vibration of Mother Earth bursting through it.

If we are attentive, we will see the liveliness in nature and experience our deepest sense of inner peace. We love the freshness and calmness surging from nature, which is why we love to be in nature or vacation in the wilderness or in the park. When we are calm and peaceful, our life is filled with bliss and happiness; food for our hearts. All we need is to find a way to redirect our attention from our fictional character to our true self to experience true happiness.

You can do this right now. Look at a plant or a tree in your vicinity and embrace its freshness and stillness. You will feel the pleasantness in the present moment, and you will experience inner peace. This inner peace is your true self and true happiness, not the happiness you accept in your rational mind based on the belief of how happiness should generally be felt.

The next chapter will discuss Einstein's wisdom about nature and a natural phenomenon that forces us to pause and dwell in our true selves.

Pause

The recent pandemic was a natural phenomenon that taught us how valuable our lives are and the benefit of pausing in our pursuit of happiness. The global ground-level ozone had dropped to a low that policymakers thought would take at least 15 years to improve sufficiently by conventional means, such as regulations. Many suffered from the pandemic, while some realized money cannot secure happiness. Also, comfort and satisfaction do not give lasting happiness.

As we discussed in the previous chapter, we can learn a lot from nature if we are open-minded and attentive to it. For that, we have to pause or stop, look around, and embrace nature. Nature provides miracles such as northern lights, rainbows, mirages, and splendid sunsets to force us to stop and dive deep into our true selves to experience inner peace. Out of those miracles, we will look into the most common for all of us, the sunset.

Sunset is a breathtaking and amazing natural phenomenon; almost anybody will stop to enjoy such a wondrous sight. When I say "stop," I mean physically and mentally, and I mean that at such moments we need to pause our constantly flowing stream of thoughts and exclude extraneous musings, just for a few moments, to focus on what has attracted our attention. Our attention will instantly be drawn to that wondrous sight and free us from all mind-created miseries. At this pause, true happiness emerges instantly.

Self-check

Consider what is likely to happen when contemplating a colorful and wondrous sunset. It may stir memories of a sunset you admired in the past, and you may recall its splendid colors clearly. Focus on the joyful moment savored as you paused in your stream of thoughts to concentrate on that wondrous sight. What is crucially important here is that pause. The magnificence of the spectacle has almost certainly made you pause longer than you did at the sight of a tree or the plant that we experimented with earlier. A significant time would have elapsed here, which is the space of calm or inner peace in you. Your rational mind lacked space and time to conceptualize anything. Hence, you experienced true happiness.

If we analyze this further, the space you recognize between thoughts is where your true happiness lies. That was in the pause before the beginning of your thoughts about the sunset. This space between every activity gives us a thought of a free moment of happiness. Once we move our attention from that space and stillness within us—the true self—the happiness we enjoy fades away. With myriad thoughts sprouting in our mind, we distract our happiness. We need to shift our attention to the space between our thoughts to experience our noble heart or true happiness.

We can practice focusing on that space to access our noble hearts. Please try the following practice and see whether you can experience inner peace—*your noble heart.*

Practice # 08: Embracing Space
*Embracing the splendor of a sunset is
relishing bliss in nature.*

Reflect on your heart's response to a colorful sunset witnessed with your pure attention. Focus with full attention on that image of the sky. What an amazing display of nature's beauty; it is so glorious that it can rob us and wipe all extraneous thoughts from our minds for one precious instant! Momentarily, inner peace will manifest in us. Our eyes may well up with tears. Embracing the beauty and color of the sunset, we might yearn to be a part of that moment and, thereby, be one with nature. At that instant, we are free from all mind-made conceptualized boundaries and discriminations. We are experiencing true happiness—true self. I am sharing my experience, and I hope you have the same.

At this point, a stray thought, such as "Do I feel this way all the time?," is likely to cut short your retreat. The next series of questions you ask may be, "Where am I? Where was I going? Why did I stop?" In other words, your mind could just urge you to go back to reading or to whatever activity you were engaged in before that blissful moment. The important point is that, for a moment, you did interrupt the stream of thoughts that dominate you, diving deep into the core of your heart, which is forever still, silent, and peaceful. That pervasive stillness prompted you to pause and keep your restlessness in check. The emerging bliss held the usual stream of thoughts at bay to experience true happiness.

You reclaimed your original state of pure attention, which you carry from birth. When you are born, you look at your surroundings without preconceived perceptions, and similarly, you open your heart to the splendor of sunset. The noble nature of your heart—*your true self*—sprouts through that openness, and you experience true happiness. When you stay in the true nature of your noble heart, it will gradually grow and enable you to evolve into a great philosopher or sage.

With this condition of spaciousness, you will clear your mind to live blissfully in the present. You have released another layer of your self-image, tainted with perceptions and concepts in your mind, and you will feel underlying peacefulness more regularly.

However, after that pause, brief or lengthy, you reconnected with your age-old habit of stream of thought passing through your mind. During the above practice, the philosopher in you may have contemplated the beauty of the spectacle and not experienced the inner space. You may have marveled at the variety of colors a sky can display. You may have enjoyed the beauty of the sky's hues—red, orange, or peach—set off by a streak of brilliant, fiery yellow, yet remained at a distance, observing the sunset as nothing but a natural phenomenon alien to your immediate life. While regarding it as something quite remote, taking place far away and of little direct relevance to you, you imagine it in your mind, which is much closer than looking at it from a distance. You might still find the setting sun interesting enough to make you pause, at least for a fraction of a second. That is your noble heart's effort to surge through your thoughts that marveled at the sunset.

Instead, such sights may trigger memories of your science lessons about the composition of the sun's rays. The more you analyze a subject, the greater the distance it creates between you and that special moment you experienced deeply for a fraction of a second. In this state of mind, questions and answers might rush to take over, forcing the blissful experience that made you pause to fade away. Then your inquiring mind predominates. The inevitable result is that you will likely move on with your life and disregard the insight you gained into the power of your noble heart. Your mind might take you away from that deeply felt moment of your true self—*inner peace.*

Our fictional character—*mind*—tries to convince us that the sun is going down at the horizon, but the truth is that Earth is rotating. Likewise, our conceptual thinking misleads us from the truth. When we go within, we realize we were taken for a ride by our fictional character. This is true for many concepts we cherish in our minds. When you set aside those concepts, you can experience your true self. I trust that now you can see the fictional character was built upon our true self.

In 1899, when the journalist John Smith interviewed Nikola Tesla, Tesla said:

"Do you know how I discovered the rotating magnetic field and induction motor which made me became famous when I was twenty-six? One summer evening in Budapest, I watched with my friend Sigetijem a sunset.

Thousands of fire was turning around in thousands of flaming colors. I remembered Faust and recited his verses, and then, as in a fog, I saw a spinning magnetic field and induction motor. I saw them in the sun!"

Tesla's great invention of reproducing electricity—*the induction motor*—came about from an open heart, not conceptual thinking. Tesla saw them in the sun when the sunset cleared his thoughts and preconceived perceptions. When you dwell in inner peace, inventions and creations are results, not activities. Without being a victim of your mind, you will use your thoughts and perceptions to propel your insight out to the world. You will use your intellect to explain your discovery. But the invention or innovation is born in your noble heart, inner peace—*your true self.*

We experience inner peace rather than understanding what it is and keeping it in memory, and I would call it experiential knowledge that Plato promoted with his work. Plato is known as perhaps the most influential philosopher of all time, providing the main opposition to the materialist view of the world.

Plato was another Greek philosopher famous for his works with his mentor, Socrates, and his student, Aristotle, during 428–347 BCE. In everyone's eyes, Plato is a great philosopher, and the greatness comes with the open mind and the nobility of heart he demonstrated in many of his works. When he said, "You can discover more about a person in an hour of play than in a year of conversation," he said that discovery is more experiential than conceptual.

In my view, Plato's statement tells us that he promoted experiential knowledge rather than logical arguments. That is why he stated that "an hour of play" is greater than "a year of conversation" to discover more about a person. So, even if the philosopher in you dominates your mind, you can be free from it and have an open mind to experience reality and learn more about a person, nature, and yourself by being with them experientially.

Here is another good assertion for experiential knowledge. I watched a documentary telecast on PBS about Jun Kaneko, a famous Japanese ceramic artist who came to the United States in 1963 at twenty-one unable to speak English. He learned English, studied, and graduated from Chouinard Art Institute in California. His work is now included in more than forty museum collections worldwide. In this documentary, he mentioned that keeping an open mind was key to his success. In his words, he is a free thinker, not scared of what others might think or say, and that gives him the gift of fearless creativity. He teaches his students by asking them to observe attentively what he is doing rather than enforcing any concept or principle of art. He wants his students to be like him and create fearlessly without any preconceived system or method.

When he refers to an "open mind," what came to my attention was a mind without conceptual thinking, not an enslaved mind—in other words, a noble heart revealed through a clouded mind. He distances his fictional character and lets his true self blossom into innovations and creations. He dwells on the noble nature of his heart—*his true self*—to innovate and create. In other words, he creates when he is "in the zone," that is, when in a state of inner peace. So, keep all mud and debris—*thoughts and perceptions*—off the lake-mind so that the pure and clear water—*bliss*—can spring from the bottom of your heart. You will then be "in the zone," which is a long pause from the myriad thoughts and confusion. That is our true self, but we build our fictional character upon it with the concepts we acquire.

Most of us follow the directions from our fictional character, and as a result, we doubt and continue to live with stress, problems, confusion, and disarray. We can distance our fictional character by recognizing the bliss within us, which surfaces from time to time and occurs when you pause, like when you stop to enjoy the wondrous sunset. In fact, you got a glimpse of it with our earlier practices. When you allow that bliss to grow in you, you can examine the depths of your heart and enter the zone or dwell in your true self. Great athletes respond in a split second, without thinking during a game, by following their intuition. When they are in the zone, they respond to intuition with no interruption from thoughts, perceptions, and fear. So, they distance themselves from their fictional character when they are in the zone. You can do the same to overcome the challenges in your life.

I trust that by now you know who you are and feel your heart's nobility—*inner peace*—at least to some extent. This nobility exists whether or not you see yourself as a philosopher or a sage. The inner peace surges through you as bliss. However, when your fictional character seeks satisfaction, your true self is obscured by many confusing thoughts and perceptions. You can go beyond your fictional character to experience your true self with your pure attention to inner peace.

As Thich Nhat Hanh aptly said in his book *Peace Is Every Step: The Path of Mindfulness in Everyday Life*: "The present moment is filled with joy and happiness. If you are attentive, you will see it."

The present moment is filled with unconceptualized joy and happiness—*in other words, with your true self.* Your true self is always joyful with inner peace, and I trust that you are experiencing it now, at least to some extent. Just focus on your inner essence right now, and feel the lightness in you. That is your true self, the noble heart, free from confusing thoughts.

We share inner peace like oxygen in the air, but until we completely dwell in it, we feel and limit it as our noble heart. When we are unaware of this, we live in our fictional character. So if you are still lost in the fictional character, you need to clear your thoughts and perceptions, and direct your pure attention to your noble heart that you experienced as pleasantness or lightness just a few minutes ago. We will discuss this further in the next chapter.

The Noble Heart

When Eckhart Tolle stated that "the primary cause of unhappiness is never the situation but your thoughts about it," in *A New Earth: Awakening to Your Life's Purpose,* he clearly pinpointed the root cause of our unhappiness. When we mull over confusing thoughts, we suffer. Unhappiness starts with overthinking and becomes a misery when it later snowballs into myriad confusing thoughts. Therefore, when looking for happiness, do not think about it; instead, turn your pure attention to the still and silent space between thoughts.

This space between thoughts is your noble heart, your true self, which is full of joy and happiness as we settle with the experiences we had in the last chapter. Our heart is full of emotions, mostly manipulated by our enslaved mind. However, our noble heart is free from all types of labeled emotions and is full of bliss. Once bliss springs from our true selves, our heart becomes noble. True happiness is that inner peace surging through our heart as bliss, which is noble. Therefore, I name it the Noble Heart.

All human beings are born with a noble heart, which is universal. Our mind, however, obscures this universal truth and creates a self-image—our fictional character. We called it the *mind*. The mind is what emotionally reacts to an external situation and mulls over it, distracting us from inner peace and identifying us as "individuals." When we do not entertain thoughts leading to the perception of self-image, our inherited bliss will surge. That is the nobility of our heart buried deep within the reservoir of inner peace. We are hardly experiencing it, since we are confined to the mind. We do not look beyond our mind; many do not know that the mind is simply another faculty. By distancing from our self-image, we can reveal the nobility of the heart and gradually travel deep into inner peace—*our true self*. You had a glimpse of the experience of your heart and inner peace by doing the practices we discussed in the last chapters. Your noble heart is the pleasantness and lightness you feel in your body and mind. This feeling is possible only if you have pure attention, free of thoughts. So, you can touch your noble heart only with pure attention. We are exploring our noble heart's universal nature—*inner peace*—as it exists within us and is fundamental to all living beings.

You can see a similar reference in the Venerable Seventeenth Karmapa's book *The Heart Is Noble: Changing the World from the Inside Out*. In the first paragraph of its first chapter, "Our Shared Ground," he states:

"Inside each of us, there is a noble heart. This heart is the source of our finest aspiration for ourselves and the world. It fills us with the courage to act on our aspirations. Our nobility may be obscured at times, covered over with small thoughts or blocked by confused and confusing emotions. But a noble heart lies intact within, each of us nonetheless, ready to open and be offered to the world ... When we clear away all that blocks it, this heart can change the world."

The above-mentioned book is a result of the author's interaction with a group of young, intelligent, American university students. It was written as an answer for the new generation and endorsed the fact that we share our noble hearts without any geographical, social, or ethnic boundaries.

Self-check

To gain an in-depth understanding of this truth, keep an open mind and recognize the response emanating from a deeper level within you as you continue to read. Do not allow your preconceived concepts and doubt to obscure the message. We need inner peace, just as we need oxygen in the air we share, to survive in this world. This sense of sharing and the peace you feel right now is your very own, and it is coming from the deepest level common to us all. Do not doubt and suppress it with your thoughts and perceptions. Let that sense of bliss come through as an inner essence. You will experience your true self—*inner peace.*

You may have experienced inner peace when you withdrew your attention from all discriminatory identities, including your gender. Experiencing means educating your heart that helps your mind; as Aristotle said, "Educating the mind without educating the heart is no education at all," which is what we discussed earlier.

We bear wisdom in our hearts and are born with this noble heart that is full of joy and happiness. When we get older, this joy and happiness is replaced by our intellect, which relies largely on information gathered from books and others' opinions. That is our self-image, which obstructs our happiness and which I call the fictional character. Therefore, as adults, we need to seek the joy and happiness that were apparent in us and enjoyed immensely in our childhood. You tasted this in earlier practices you tried, and I trust that you now recognize your noble heart to some extent.

As humans, we are meant to be aware of many things in us and our surroundings, including our minds. Modern humans are known as *Homo sapiens, sapiens,* because we are wise enough to know that we have a thinking mind, which means we can distinguish our mind from our heart.

Homo sapiens, not *Homo sapiens, sapiens,* were always victims of their minds, and they could not separate their hearts from their minds and could not understand that the mind is another faculty that we can use as a tool. Once we recognize the difference between heart and mind, we become *Homo sapiens, sapiens,* per the classification of modern humans. So here we are, testing which side of human evolution we are on, either *Homo sapiens* or *Homo sapiens, sapiens,* who know that the mind is a tool to use for our benefit rather than become a victim of it.

When we say *heartfelt,* our attention recognizes the incident without preconceived thoughts or perceptions. Instead of going with heartfelt intuition, we often act on our mind's direction to become *Homo sapiens.* If we keep our attention on our blissful noble heart, we will be drawn to inner peace effortlessly, which is our true self. We will be elevated from *Homo sapiens* to *Homo sapiens, sapiens* who know our true selves. When our attention flows through into our deeper levels, we feel more and more intense pleasantness, labeled with different words at different degrees of feelings, as illustrated below:

Pure attention /Awareness

Noble Heart / Blissfulness

Inner Peace / True Happiness / True self

The above words are different concepts and have abstract interpretations in our minds. Based on rational thinking, we assign different meanings to each word and cling to it. In other words, the same word can give a different meaning according to your interpretation. Our enslaved mind does that, and we must distance ourselves from that thought process. We use words to direct us toward the idea or the experience behind the word. Once we understand one word, our attention should follow the meaning deeper, and this deeper meaning may be labeled with a different word. Follow the above process to take your attention deeper in order to experience your true self with those commonly used sets of words to describe your experiences.

Our fictional characters always try to confuse us and bring misery and disarray to our lives. We can be aware of this, but we may not know how to deal with it. We may temporarily suppress our thought-related feelings, but they will resurface without any warning. In contrast, our heart loves peace and bliss; when you dwell in your heart, you experience true happiness without lapse. I trust that you navigated these experience levels down to the noble heart with the practices you have done so far. If you have done the practices correctly, you should be able to hold on to that experience effortlessly.

Have you ever wondered why our eyes get wet when we feel joy or sorrow? On one occasion, I observed a physically challenged person's difficulty getting into a wheelchair. My help was accepted with gratitude, as evidenced by the person's expression—tears in their eyes—and appreciation conveyed by the words "Thank you!" The impact of the incident on me was quite amazing. Unremarkable though it was, it brought bliss to my heart, joy to my mind, and tears to the eyes of both of us. That little episode made an incredibly powerful impression on both the person and myself! The social and physical differences of free nobility, dormant in our hearts, generated such bliss within that its impact caused our eyes to well up with tears.

This could be interpreted as an unremarkable incident. Instead, reconsider the situation: a person who needed help appreciated my help and expressed gratitude after the help was rendered—*but it's worth considering what's really happening here more deeply*. The instinctive response—*tears*—is not a biological process triggered by preconceived perceptions; it is an expression of the noble nature of our hearts. We did not push that with thoughts or past experiences; tears surged within us effortlessly.

Many modern-day sages expressed their blissful experience from the noble heart to tears. In their experience, they were surprised to see eyes brimming with tears and wet cheeks after emerging from meditative states and relating that to their blissful experience during the meditation. I experience this regularly, and many confess to having the same experience.

However, one can also interpret this as a bodily reaction through certain hormonal changes that surface through the eyes in the form of tears. That is your gathered knowledge or intellectual interpretation, and a common philosopher may concur with that idea.

A sage may offer an entirely different interpretation of the same incident. A sage interprets the tears as a stream of bliss evoked in the noble heart of each person's inner essence. A sage sees the tears as an expression of the heart's nobility. This nobility is inherent in the hearts of people and it leads them to exchange their innermost uniqueness, which proves that the heart is noble and common to all. Tears are merely a physical manifestation of joy and happiness—bliss—an expression of the noble nature of the heart.

After searching and mulling over many subjects, philosophers find their inner peace—*the nobility of the heart*—deep within. Instead, you can direct your attention to your noble heart when your eyes are welling up. To experience this phenomenon, try the following practice.

Practice # 09: Recognizing the Noble Heart
An incident in your life that moved you to tears
expresses your noble heart.

First, clear your mind and get pure attention by using any earlier practices. You may be skillful enough to instantly bring up your pure attention with the intense experiences gained from those practices.

Once you have done that, try recalling an incident in your life that moved you to tears. It does not have to be a happy one. You may, for instance, have wept when you lost someone close to you. I suggest you focus on that moment of grief and try recalling the intuitive feelings you experienced at that time. They may be dormant, but they are still within you and will rise to the surface if you allow it. That heartfelt moment boiling inside may impact you in the same or a much stronger way than on the day you first felt it, and the result would be tears, or at least a feeling of sorrow. This emotion of sorrow breaks your heart, and tears surge to comfort you. These tears manifest your inner peace, trying to calm you down. It is the same as lamenting when you hear about a tragedy in your neighborhood or anywhere in the world. Such an incident shatters the underlying peace that holds this universe. This is our noble heart for you and me, but collectively, it is inner peace.

If you find the above difficult, then try to recall a joyful moment. At that time, you would have felt like a child who enjoys inner unity, unaware of all physical and social differences. Try to dwell in that joyful moment and experience the joy and bliss you had then. This experience is not your gathered knowledge; these are the experiences that reside in your heart. Stay with this notion as long as you can. You will touch your noble heart, manifesting as tears in your eyes.

Practice this a few times to see whether you can embrace your heart at a deeper level. Make this a habit whenever you are alone and have time. I experience that stillness and pleasantness through me frequently. You may do this while in bed if you have trouble sleeping. Make sure you are not becoming a victim of your mind. You must clear your mind and be ardent with pure attention to start this practice.

The above practice directly takes you to your noble heart. As mentioned earlier, this is your pure attention at a deeper level. You touched this level when the original incident happened. But your mind did not allow you to sustain it. Since now you have experienced it again, you can surely sustain your attention much longer than then. With this, you will touch your noble heart.

In brief, we are aware of the soft corner within us, which is our inherited compassion as human beings. We often ignore this corner, since we live in a fictional character and lack pure attention. The soft corner in us surfaces from time to time, regardless of the joyful or sorrowful situation in which we find our deeper essence. At the surface level, we can see this when a mass-scale disaster occurs anywhere in the world. Then our true self expands to the whole of humanity. The devastation is shared with compassion by almost everyone. Many weep together and go to the extent of volunteering time and resources with compassion. We need to recognize this as the universal, yet unique, nature of the noble heart or inner peace in every human being at a deeper level. I hope you can see what I refer to as pure attention to the noble heart; then, the noble heart connects to inner peace. I use this equation because, when it comes to inner peace, only with attention clear of any thoughts or perceptions—*pure attention*—can you connect with it. When you are free from thoughts and perceptions, there is no interpretation to differentiate your attention from the noble heart, inner peace, or true self.

Pure attention

Noble Heart

Inner Peace / True Self

As depicted above, we can conceptualize these as three deeper levels within us. However, when you experience them free from perceptions, you do not feel differentiated levels or layers. You cannot assign different labels, but you experience your attention expanding to a wider space, through your body and beyond. It is like when you drop some object onto still water, circles of ripples spread on the surface. Your pure attention spreads from your body and mind to the surrounding space and beyond. You will blend with inner peace in nature like ripples die down in the water at the wider circle.

Whether a king or a commoner, the richest or the poorest, this inner peace is something we do share, universally. Some call this a universal energy field, but I prefer to call it inner peace, which is true happiness. At the same time, it is unique to each of us when seen through the mind. Therefore, it is difficult to recognize, or it might only be seen with limitations and as our noble heart. To our mind, inner peace is the nobility of our heart. We need to move our attention from our thoughts to our noble hearts to recognize inner peace when it surfaces within us in the form of tears.

Therefore, please keep an open mind without conceptualized doubts, and be wisely attentive to the intuition sparks within you while reading this book. This intuition is very important to any circumstance in life, as it is for our well-being. When we encounter compassion and empathy, equanimity stems from our inner essence; we should not doubt it or let it slip away from our attention. We must be vigilant for all signs and signals coming from our noble heart to make our life blissful and happy. Our enslaved mind brings thoughts, perceptions, doubt, and fear of those signs. It creates our ever-changing self-image, disguising the deepest level of our universal nature with receptivity to inner peace.

Whatever you learn through your heartfelt experiences is truly intelligent. If you conceptualize based on your thought process, it is a subjective intellect that can change with your fleeting thoughts and perceptions. You practice recognizing your true self and experiencing the nobility of your heart by being with nature and digging into your past experiences.

You may presume that you are a sage, capable of looking into the depths of the heart, often to recognize the peace within. You may be fascinated with the silence of the dawn, and enjoy the calm and the chirping of birds as the only disturbance to inner peace. You may be a person who meditates a few times and sees yourself as a saint. You may be a priest who imagines yourself as a sage or close to becoming one. You may pause before a tree or gaze at the sunset and relax for a while, feeling satisfied and thinking you have touched inner peace. You may be a good meditation practitioner teaching others how to meditate, or you may be someone in between all those self-images. However, as long as the concept of satisfaction takes precedence in your mind, your self-image remains. If so, neither meditation nor priesthood alone will transform you into a great sage; you are still living in your fictional character.

Now we know our noble heart and the fictional character, but we need to go beyond our self-image to experience our true self.

Part III

What Is Beyond Self-Image?

Pure Attention

As I mentioned earlier, we are born with alertness, which we carry throughout our lives until we die. We also call it attention, awareness, or consciousness. However, some scholars and academics may see slight differences in these words, but I do not. Although dictionaries provide accurate and wide usage of a word, any word holds a unique meaning for each of us. This applies not only to words; anything in this world has a different meaning for each of us. That is because our concepts are unique to us, depending on our thoughts and perceptions. However, the alertness we are born with is the same for all of us. We don't see and feel that until we go beyond our self-image—our fictional character.

Our hearts can exist in a variety of different realms. When our attention is lost in our thoughts and perceptions, we stimulate emotions, then feel sorrow or joy. Then our heart is in the realm of concepts and thoughts, where we feel anger, sorrow, and sometimes satisfaction. But when we pay pure attention to the pleasantness in us—*our heart's nobility*—we are directly connected with our true selves.

We recognize our true selves if we are attentive to the noble heart. We can see everything happening around us as mere vibrations or fleeting changes. Thoughts, perceptions, and emotions disturb our noble hearts, our inner peace. And when our attention is vested in the vibrations created by our thoughts and perceptions, we suffer. We move away from such suffering when we wisely redirect our attention back to our true selves. With pure attention, we can dwell in inner peace and live blissfully.

The purpose here is simply to provide an appropriate practice to ensure a more in-depth understanding of what I mean by pure attention. I use pure attention as the first step to recognizing our innermost essence — *the noble heart*. It matures into a blissful feeling when you keep your pure attention free from thoughts, residing instead in the noble nature of your heart. Some call the expression of the heart "gut feelings," referencing intuition that comes from our innermost essence.

Self-check

In the early days, I used to have a calculator with an alarm on it, and I would set the alarm for every hour, when it would stop after three chimes. I used this as a reminder to pause from too much thinking and return to pure attention for a minute or two. You may try this, too. If you make this practice a habit, you will constantly dwell in your noble heart and have intense pure attention. Then inner peace is inevitable. Inner peace, common to the whole universe, is your noble heart that you see through your pure attention, your true self.

Recently, I read about the approach of the philosopher and author Joseph Campbell, who lived from 1904 to 1987. He was an American professor of literature at Sarah Lawrence College and worked in comparative mythology and comparative religion. In his works, he covered many aspects of the human experience. His philosophy has been summarized by his often-repeated phrase, "Follow your bliss." He stated the following in his book *The Power of Myth:*

"If you follow your bliss, you put yourself on a kind of track that has been there all the while, waiting for you, and the life that you ought to be living is the one you are living. Wherever you are—if you are following your bliss, you are enjoying that refreshment, that life within you, all the time."

He confesses that he derived this idea from the *Upanishads*—an ancient Sanskrit text—by stating the following:

"Now, I came to this idea of bliss because, in Sanskrit, which is the great spiritual language of the world, there are three terms that represent the brink, the jumping-off place to the ocean of transcendence: Sat-Chit-Ananda. The word 'Sat' means being. 'Chit' means consciousness. 'Ananda' means bliss or rapture. I thought, 'I don't know whether my consciousness is proper consciousness or not; I don't know whether what I know of my being is my proper being or not, but I do know where my rapture is. So, let me hang on to rapture, and that will bring me both my consciousness and my being.' I think it worked."

His method resembles our journey to our true selves. Here, we employ pure attention, which leads to our noble heart—*the bliss*—that puts us on a path to inner peace. When Campbell said, "you are enjoying that refreshment, that life within you, all the time," he referred to inner peace.

This path has been waiting for us, leading to the life we should live from birth. The two fundamental obstacles to this are friction and clinging created by our thoughts and perceptions. When we usher in our bliss with pure attention, those obstacles will fade away, and the pathway to being alive will open for us. We will return to the state of blissfulness we are born with and experience our true selves.

You may have read several books on being happy and transcendence to your true self. Their messages may be vivid, and you may have difficulty conceptualizing and comprehending them. The fundamental error you are making is trying to understand a phenomenon beyond your intellect. My effort here is to take you through an experiential journey rather than adding another concept to your memory bank.

You may have a concept of what bliss feels like and want to follow that concept, which is not what Campbell did. He found the bliss clear of thoughts and concepts, and followed it.

We need to do the same. I take you to three deeper levels of experiences beyond your conceptual thinking in this journey to inner peace, which is the best way to share my experience with you.

We are aware of anything and everything happening around us but not the nature of our inner self. So, set aside your concept for the word *awareness* and replace it with *pure attention*. Our first deeper experience level is to pay attention to the inner landscape. Rather than thinking about it, "pure attention" is what you do. I put that into an equation:

$$Pure\ Attention = Awareness$$

Similarly, when Campbell said, "Follow your bliss," many concepts about bliss may come to your mind instead of experiencing it in your heart. Therefore, to distance you from the concept of bliss, I would like you to experience it as the nature of your heart. You frequently experience this blissful nature of your heart, but your mind ignores or misinterprets it to keep you away from true happiness. When your pure attention matures, the deeper level of your experience becomes blissful; that is the noble heart you were born with. So, the second deeper level of experience we get in this wondrous journey is Noble Heart, free from the concept of bliss. Which I depict as:

$$Noble\ Heart = Blissfulness$$

Generally, our mind does not allow us to experience bliss in our heart. Our mind takes us to other emotions, like anger, sorrow, excitement, and satisfaction with our thoughts and concepts to obscure blissfulness. We need to be cautious of this. We feel inner peace if we pause thinking and focus on a thoughts-free space, as you experienced in earlier practices. Then you are following your bliss, the noble heart. The noble heart is beyond our conceptual thinking and emotions. When you dwell in your noble heart, you experience inner peace. You may have a certain concept about happiness, and please let go of that concept and be prepared to experience it as inner peace. That means:

Inner Peace = True Happiness

Depending on the degree of attention you have developed so far, you may fall into the ocean of inner peace right now, due to the different stages of experiences you gain through the practices outlined in this book. You now know your approach to life and which path you have chosen to travel along this journey. Or else, if you are a person on the brink of transcendence, you will fall into the ocean of inner peace by keeping your pure attention on blissfulness.

When Joseph Campbell asked you to follow your bliss, he meant following the noble nature of your heart. The word *Ananda* in ancient Sanskrit scriptures means the ecstatic experience of being alive. You experience this irrespective of your age and physical and mental conditions. Flashback to your younger age and look for a difference in your soul between then and now. You cannot see any difference in yourself at the deeper level, then and now. You may think you are old, but still, you feel the same child at the core of your heart. That is your Ananda which has been translated into English as bliss or rapture. You experience it all the time but do not pay attention to it. Once you begin to pay attention and recognize the unshakable noble heart—inner peace—you experience the bliss of being alive—true happiness. I find that tears are the physical manifestation of unshakable inner peace. See whether you can experience it by doing the following practice.

Practice # 10: Experiencing Pure Attention
Any intense moment brings about pure attention.

At this stage, you should be well aware of pure attention. Once again, try to dwell in—not dwell on—a joyful moment you can recall. You should have the same results, a pleasant feeling in you, clear of thought. You were joyful, without interruptions from any thoughts or perceptions, and experiencing the bliss of being alive! Hence, the mind does not influence your true self. You are experiencing pure attention.

A similar experience can come when you are drowning or ecstatic. Any intense moment distances your mind from your true self, and your pure attention will surge. You can try this by taking a deep breath and holding it as long as possible. You will feel the intense need to let go of your breath in a few minutes, to be free from that hold. In such a moment, you may recognize your pure attention apart from your self-image, pleading to release that breath. Then, let go of that breath while focusing on relief running through your body and mind with pure attention. Relax in that feeling for a few minutes.

I trust that you can experience this intense awareness right now: pure attention to your true self. This time, you may clearly notice the difference between your thinking mind—intellect—and the noble heart—intelligence.

I find that pure attention has a much closer meaning to everybody than talking about happiness, blissfulness, or a noble heart. But at the same time, please do not forget that those words describe the deeper levels of pure attention.

Our true self is pure attention, free of thoughts and perceptions, and it is also the key to true happiness. Beyond our self-image, our true self exists as pure attention; some refer to this as consciousness or soul. For our journey to inner peace, I would like to refer to our true self as our pure attention. When we say consciousness, it can be tainted by many concepts, not pure as our true selves.

However, we might believe that satisfactory answers to all our chaos can be found. When seeking satisfaction, however, you are a victim of your mind and pursuing happiness from outside. You may feel satisfied with a new thing you bought, thinking it will make you happy. In the following chapters, we will explore satisfaction and happiness to recognize their relevance to our well-being and true self.

Satisfaction

For most people, happiness is a fleeting satisfaction. Your self-image always looks for satisfaction and thinks it makes you happy. We need to recognize that happiness should be lasting pleasantness rather than short-lived satisfaction based on fleeting perceptions. Our perceptions result from the memories and concepts we entertain with thoughts inside our self-image or mind. When you think, "I am old" or "I am young," you become old or young as you have perceived it in your mind. Likewise, we seek satisfaction based on our perceptions. Recalling previous experiences or memories that gave birth to the original perception, we instantly seek more satisfaction. Therefore, satisfaction is relative to our perceived state of mind. But true happiness is blissful and free of fleeting perceptions.

When you think, it is your mind that engages in the process. Therefore, according to your perceptions, your needs and wants are created within the boundaries of your mind. These perceptions result from the analysis or questions you entertained earlier, and they direct your mind to seek satisfaction based on memories. Your satisfaction level may vary depending on your perception of needs or wants. As you know by now, those perceptions are not really yours. They are built upon perceptions you accumulated from others' opinions and external stimuli. None of them are what your heart wants or needs. They are what others want and need. Your heart needs peacefulness and wants to be happy. Therefore, you should distance yourself from the mind-made chaos, including your pursuit of satisfaction.

I hope you have already noticed that thinking or seeking satisfaction won't bring lasting happiness. If you allow yourself to probe deeper, you will conclude that the satisfaction gained in that way does not give you the peace of mind or happiness you sought in the first place. Once you are satisfied with one thing, you seek another, looking for greater satisfaction. You can never be happy in your pursuit of fleeting satisfaction, and such pursuit is a trick of your fictional character to keep you away from your true self. Therefore, satisfaction is within your self-image, not beyond it.

Self-check

Reflect on the satisfaction you have sought so far in your life as a self-check. For instance, is it as fulfilling as you had imagined? You may think you have everything you want. Still, are you truly happy with your life? In your desire to save the planet, you may assume that the target of your quest is, indeed, noble. But if you think deeply enough, in retrospect, you might realize that what you really want is to shape your self-image. In that case, having changed what you perceived as wrong, you would proudly proclaim, "I did this" or "I changed that." But your rudimentary motive would have been to satisfy yourself by claiming victory. Is that satisfaction truly noble, and does it bring lasting happiness? The act of fulfilling your needs, the kind you consider helpful to your life or the life of others, generates self-centered satisfaction. It is not true happiness. I hope you agree with me on this.

Many people believe in spending money and time, doing good deeds, expecting merit, satisfaction, or recognition out of fear of consequences after death. If this is the case, you are ultimately looking for satisfaction. As long as you expect something in return, doing such good deeds is a trick of your mind, and you are looking for self-satisfaction. You cannot get true happiness by doing such things while expecting something in return. Instead, these actions should come from your heart. If you do your good deed that way, your heart will fill with bliss and cause your eyes to well up with tears. That is true happiness.

The mind pursues satisfaction at every moment but often fails to achieve it. In some cases, such satisfaction may be low or even nonexistent. If so, this probably means that seeking satisfaction concerns your self-image. Driven by its lack of success in attaining the highest satisfaction levels, the mind persists in its quest.

This pursuit resembles the approach of philosophers who seek answers to every question; thwarted in their efforts, they end up asking more questions in their perennial quest. This pursuit brings stress and unhappiness, and the miseries created through this process never end. Since we seek happiness through fleeting satisfaction, we get quite the opposite: unhappiness.

We cling to the conceptual desire or craving for social status, comfort, lust, and even peace, and we seek satisfaction. These are our longings, born through clinging to thoughts and perceptions externally and internally throughout our lives. Your search for higher social status by clinging to the perception of what others may think of you is an external longing. Your looking for comfort by changing your pillow with the perception that it will satisfy you is an internal longing. In either case, that comfort will last only a few minutes and will lead you to seek more comfort, and in the end, it will make you unhappy.

The famous British philosopher John Stuart Mill, who lived in the nineteenth century, believed in simplicity when it came to happiness. Mill was a proponent of utilitarianism and adopted the ancient Greeks' wisdom. Instead of inundating his life with desire, he believed in using things for a purpose, and if they served no purpose, if they were not needed, he banished them from his life. His famous saying, "I have learned to seek my happiness by limiting my desires, rather than in attempting to satisfy them," comes from self-actualization. We try to be happy by satisfying our mundane or noble desires. Happiness is always far away within an enslaved mind, and satisfaction seems much closer, and we pursue it by clinging to our fleeting thoughts and perceptions. As Mill discovered, limiting the pursuit of satisfaction itself brings true happiness.

We will settle in, or cease seeking, when we realize that satisfying desires does not make us happy. Neither any material fulfillment nor achievements of any kind brings us lasting happiness. You may have heard about many unsatisfied scholars, millionaires, addicts, activists, or anyone in between who are now seeking happiness elsewhere, such as in ancient teachings or spiritual practices.

The mind is indeed the creator of many things in this world. The human mind is meant to support our intuition, and in doing so, it creates many things to help us. Often, the result falls short of the goal since perceptions get in the way. As you already know, the mind does not cease its effort; it keeps creating things, some of which are helpful and others harmful to lives on this planet. In brief, satisfaction is subjective and short-lived since it formulates within our minds. Satisfaction lasts until your next perception. Our perceptions change rapidly because their basis is our fleeting thoughts.

We need to cultivate the habit of observing the self-image more often by identifying the bliss in us and following it to dwell in inner peace. Instead of climbing every mountain, it is as though we should marvel at the surrounding beauty of the sky from the valley of our self-landscape. Until we evolve to that level by uplifting our attention—*pure attention*—the self-image will continue to form within the enslaved mind. We will be in the never-ending pursuit of satisfaction.

Therefore, we need to abandon our pursuit to experience true happiness. I hope you will experience this with the following practice.

Practice # 11: Abandoning the Pursuit
Look inwardly to pause your pursuit to experience true happiness.

Before trying the earlier practices, had you ever focused on your inner longing other than to change your appearance to impress others? You may have asked for others' opinions on choosing your clothes, house, and partner. Most people look outwardly to seek happiness, which is a self-centered approach to satisfy their minds rather than be truly happy.

I trust that you are now skillful enough to move your attention from your thoughts to the space in between them. Focus on where your body aches and mindfully relax that area. Your ache will change to pleasantness. Then scan your whole body and relax the tightness in each body part. Let go of that tightness to notice how physically peaceful and happy you are. Your heart will fill with bliss, and a smile may appear on your face! When I guide meditation, I wait until all participants relax their bodies and a smile appears on their faces effortlessly. That is my measurement of whether they are ready for the next step. It will help you relax until you are ready for the next step.

Then, focus on your passing thoughts and bring your attention to the space between them. Sustain your attention there and notice that space gradually widening inside you. You will sense that space's silent and still nature, the inner peace dormant within you. This inner peace is there from your birth, but you have probably never looked for it. Instead, you were busy satisfying the opinions of others, thinking that would bring happiness to you. When the space between your thoughts widens, your mind gets to relax, too. Your mind and body are relaxed and ready to experience true happiness at this stage. You have abandoned the pursuit. From here onward, you do not have to do anything. Keep your pure attention on experiencing what is happening in that ever-widening space. If you do this right and persistently for a while, you will experience the phenomenon beyond your self-image.

Try this practice and bring your attention to the space between the thoughts, to settle in your true self before addressing any challenging situation. With this practice, you open your mind and look inwardly to abandon your pursuit of satisfaction. You identify inner peace and experience true happiness.

Many philosophers will continue to think and question until they realize that conceptual wisdom alone is not worthy. Then they turn inward to see answers. This can become a reality because great philosophers are prepared to recognize opposites and are willing to keep an open mind. Their inward approach refuses to be constrained by fleeting perceptions or the desire for mere satisfaction. However, as amateur philosophers driven by desire and ego, many of us could not do this. We cling to the thoughts and perceptions that uplift our self-image — ego. Great philosophers, however, are open-minded, free of prejudice, and try not to cling to any specific ideal. In other words, they focus on observing the self-image from a higher ground to become a bearer of wisdom instead of seeking it.

Unawareness of the difference between the heart and mind distinguishes you from a great philosopher or sage. You believe that science and your mind have a satisfying answer to every question. But I trust that you can go beyond your memories and perceptions to experience true happiness. Many scientists like Einstein and philosophers like Socrates lived beyond their self-images. However, it is temporary because you cannot stop thinking. Sooner or later, your mind will begin to ask more questions and seek satisfaction again on a subject you believed you had all the answers to. This will continue until you realize that satisfaction is not the happiness you pursue. This pursuit will stop when you become a great philosopher or sage who sees the world through inner peace without lapses.

You have already experienced this condition for a fraction of a second when you stopped to admire a colorful sunset in the previous practices and you, hopefully, experienced true happiness beyond satisfaction. Similarly, when you pause to gaze at a tree, you feel the bliss springing up and experience the peace and calm within you. During these experiences, you may have realized that thinking or seeking satisfaction is not the ultimate purpose of life. This insight is not a conceptual understanding but an experiential one. If you allow yourself to probe deeper, you will conclude that satisfaction does not give you the peace of mind you seek. Then you will stop pursuing satisfaction, see the world through inner peace, and be happy.

It's not as if a sage is immune to being carried away by the momentary satisfaction derived from a particular sight or object. However, the time lost in seeking further satisfaction will be considerably limited in such cases. Because, sooner or later, the sage's noble heart will catch the mind in its trick of offering momentary satisfaction, which distracts from the blissfulness. In that sense, a sage must dwell in inner peace to recognize every source of satisfaction as just another aspect of a mind game. Once you have a similar experience with your practices, you will continue to live without being swayed by the mind's allure. In other words, every second of your life will be blissful when you learn to dwell in your true self.

If you are the kind of person who occasionally gets carried away by the short-lived pleasure of satisfaction but recognizes such satisfaction is not happiness, then you are a sage. It means you have a sense of peace that dwells within you, which is attributable to your openness and receptivity to bliss. Perhaps, until now, you neither noticed nor recognized this as an expression of the nobility of your heart. After trying some of the practices I have introduced so far, I sincerely hope that you will be able to distinguish between momentary satisfaction and the existence of bliss, which is true happiness.

Interestingly, we will be happy when we are far from our fictional characters and go beyond our self-image. Our happiness doesn't come from external rewards or praises. The external delights based on perceptions may satisfy us for a few minutes, hours, or days, but they cannot make us happy. I am sure you already know that; this is just a reminder.

So, satisfaction is not the condition we find beyond self-image. It could be happiness, and I find that the meaning behind the word *happiness* may differ from person to person We will further examine happiness in the next chapter.

Happiness

By now, you may have clearly established that happiness and satisfaction lie at opposite ends of the continuum of pleasantness. Happiness comes from the heart through the openness of the mind. On the other hand, satisfaction is always driven by short-lived perceptions. When questions go unanswered or cravings are not satisfied, the result will be unhappiness, frustration, or an unsatisfactory outcome. But true happiness does not involve thoughts or perceptions when it permeates your inner being. Instead, happiness neither fulfills nor discounts your needs or cravings; it wipes them out and fills you with bliss. It is independent of your cravings or needs, unconcerned with their satisfaction or the lack thereof, and free of stress or depression. Therefore, happiness is not a self-centered ever-changing phenomenon like satisfaction. True happiness is universal and available for everyone to experience at will.

If you pursue fleeting happiness, you will never arrive at happiness because you are looking for it intellectually rather than being with it. True happiness is not conventional pleasure or satisfaction based on perceptions. True happiness is a sense of bliss that comes from your core; when your attention is free from distractions, you will experience this clearly. In other words, happiness occurs when you are free from all distractions, especially when you evade friction and the clinging coming from your enslaved mind. Our true happiness is free from inner agitations and irritations that can bother us, irrespective of our life circumstances. Whether as material things or metaphysical longings, things we accumulate throughout our life cannot make us happy.

When true happiness arises, you don't perceive any concern over satisfaction or dissatisfaction. Happiness occupies your mind completely, and there is no room to think about any of that. You find true happiness beyond your self-image. You will realize that everything arises and ceases based on your thoughts and perceptions. While it seems improbable to come across individuals who find themselves in this state and lead blissful and happy lives, it is not as rare as you may think. There is intense happiness in each of us that we call bliss, what we've been calling the nobility of our heart. We need to elevate this bliss to go beyond our self-image and live with true happiness.

Self-check

Since reading this book, I sincerely hope you have experienced blissful moments that have preserved your sanity. Therefore, you can work on uplifting your happiness with enough mental equilibrium to explore your true self sufficiently. Whether philosopher or sage, perhaps you have yet to become aware that you bear the bliss that brings lasting happiness. Often, human beings fail to recognize true happiness but appreciate and enjoy it nevertheless, mistaking it for short-lived satisfaction.

For example, you may take a vacation, thinking it will satisfy you, but you're really looking for true happiness. If you prefer amusement parks or vibrant activities for your vacation, you may be looking for perceived happiness. In other words, you are pursuing satisfaction rather than happiness. Suppose you prefer sightseeing and enjoy being in nature to admire the beauty of natural phenomena. In that case, you really seek a blissful time for peace of mind and true happiness, not satisfaction. You are approaching your life with the sage in you, and you are much closer to inner peace than a philosopher who seeks satisfaction.

Whether humans recognize it or not, inner peace is certainly a phenomenon that exists everywhere. Often lost in our thoughts, we become enslaved by our minds and mistakenly think we are happy. We fail to recognize the bliss in our hearts, even when it surfaces occasionally. Bliss surfaces only when we are able to cut off all thoughts and pause for a moment, as we do while gazing at a tree or admiring the beauty of a sunset. These sights that move us to joy and tears are clear examples of the bliss in our noble hearts and manifest themselves through us. These events bring us to the question of whether the noble heart itself is the bliss that exists, regardless of whether humans feel that or not. It is a question that many individuals have pondered in the past. And irrespective of whether they were philosophers or sages, their interest in the subject impelled them to investigate it thoroughly. In the process, they discovered universal blissfulness—*inner peace*. You are becoming one of them as you read this book and practice the exercises. When our pure attention goes beyond our self-image, we settle in inner peace. Therefore, inner peace is what you find beyond your self-image. This is your true self.

You are not an individual self or self-image but only a blissful sensation—inner peace.

Self-Image

When you examine the above image, what do you see? A face bearing a peaceful expression or an incomplete sketch? Inquiring philosophers see a sketch yet to be completed, while the sage in you infers the peace depicted in that same sketch. While looking at this image, pause for a moment, just as you would stop and admire a colorful sunset. Initially, you may not notice the incompleteness of the sketch because you are focused on its peaceful expression. That is your heart's intuition. The peaceful expression of the drawing resembles inner peace, and a stream of bliss will flow within you as a response. However, in the very next second, your mind plays its usual tricks and obstructs your bliss with the perception that the picture is "incomplete." If you do not see the peacefulness depicted in this image, at least for a couple of seconds, philosophical concepts are prominent in you. You may need to work on the upcoming practices carefully.

Self-check

Now, as a self-check, contemplate one of your friend's faces. Please try to see through their facial image and recognize the inner peace in them. If you have already established your inner peace, you will see their inner peace irrespective of what facial impression they present. I see that inner peace in every person I meet, irrespective of whether this is a familiar person or a total stranger. Inner peace radiates through our liveliness. Some call this our aura, which sometimes reflects inner peace. Some people have shattered auras. I have felt this at times. This aura feels like a heavy wind going with them when they pass by. You may have experienced this too. Therefore, I do not call inner peace an aura, but it is a serene simile.

The image of a face also symbolizes the profound truth of the universal nature of inner peace. The face takes its shape from the surrounding frame. The black lines within are similar to the way our thoughts formulate perceptions, contribute to our persona, and define our character. Without the presence of the black color, we cannot recognize a face or even an image in the white space. If undisturbed by thoughts, emotions, and perceptions, our inner essence is blissful, peaceful, and pristine, like the white space. Bliss shines in us like the color white emanating through the sketch of the face. Our inner essence is shared with others, like the vast white space sharing pictures, words, and sentences on this page.

The absence of black color, other than the words, is a simile for the thought-free bliss you experience from time to time. But mostly, the black lines catch your attention, just like your thoughts, perceptions, emotions, and seeking of satisfaction take precedence over your blissful essence—*your true self*. We surrender to our self-image because we lack attentiveness to inner peace. So enslaved do we become by the mental processes that we fail to appreciate the beauty and brilliance of the white surface—*the true self*—that provides the base for our self-image. Similarly, the pursuit of satisfaction blinds you from the beauty and significance of your base—*inner peace*. Allow your inner peace to rise to the surface to experience true happiness. Spend a few minutes gazing at the blank surface between the letters and words on this page. You will see brilliant space surging through them. So much so that you see only the blank surface. That will give you the clarity of vision necessary to appreciate your inner essence. In the sketch, black represents the mind, and white represents the happiness dormant within us, inner peace, and our true self.

We use our own approach when interpreting the above image of the face. Philosophers start from the image drawn with black ink and later notice the white background—*inner peace*—that gives birth to it. On the other hand, sages see the white background with clarity and notice the black ink forming a peaceful expression, the image of a peaceful face.

You can recognize the peace and tranquility within you, undisturbed by emotional upheaval. It is imperative that we recognize this special moment, in which we experience the expression of our true selves.

The more we recognize the bliss within, the more we enhance our receptivity to our true self. Sometimes you may feel you've done enough thinking and need a break, perhaps by going to a park or on vacation. This urge stems from your heart to remind you to be with inner peace, and I call this urge a type of encouragement or longing for happiness. Many of us misinterpret this longing and look for fleeting satisfaction. Underlying this urge for complete mental relaxation is our longing to be happy. I would not call this longing a desire for satisfaction since it is not conceptual seeking. But we often let our perceptions suppress our longing and introduce other priorities, mostly supported by doubt and fear.

Explore within by frequently recognizing the bliss abiding in you. It is like pure, clean water flowing in from an open faucet while emptying out the dirty water from the sink. Your yearning to enjoy bliss will push away all the thoughts leading to doubt and misery, and it will cleanse your mind. Eventually, bliss will fill your mind and body like clear water fills the sink, and you will experience true happiness. That is what will happen when you do the following practice.

Practice # 12: Beyond Our Self-Image
True happiness exists beyond our self-image.

Our fictional characters are at work when we look around and chat with others. Therefore, close your eyes, and spend a few seconds probing your pure attention deep into the inner silence. Try to relax and recognize the calm and peaceful nature within yourself. You should be able to do this quickly since you have previous experience in similar practices. Spread that pleasant feeling to the space within and around you. Allow this unconditional awareness and the arising calmness and happiness to embrace you. You are experiencing true happiness. This true happiness exists free from the interference of the enslaved mind, in other words, the self-image. What you did just now allows bliss to occupy you more fully, and it will create concept-free enthusiasm for inner peace. With such blissful courage, you disregard fear or fearful consequences. Your true self is this fearless space of liveliness. I refer to this condition as the bliss of being alive—true happiness. I hope you get the same experience as I constantly do.

It is like going to a vehicle crash site to rescue injured victims without hesitation or fear: You defeat the tricks of the fictional character and go to the danger zone with courage that is not subject to any preconceived perceptions of fear. Every situation in your life could be like a crash site that you will face without hesitation, fear, or doubt. You will experience the bliss of being alive: true happiness. True happiness is the inner peace in and around us, clear of our mind-created doubt and fear.

Once I was at a restaurant where the chef came to our table and cooked our meal. While preparing the food, the chef demonstrated his cookery and acrobatic skills. He tossed up eggs without breaking them and shot the cooked ones onto our plates. Then he soaked his finger with oil and lit it to amuse his audience. He challenged me to do the same. Without hesitation, I put my index finger into the oil jar and allowed him to light it up for the amusement of himself and the rest of the people in the restaurant. I kept my finger pointing up as he did, and the oil burnt out without burning my skin.

Later, when I contemplated the incident, I realized that I acted without thinking, and it did not occur to me that my finger would burn. So I did not fear and doubt. I went by my heart's intuition without any interruption from my enslaved mind!

Subsequently, I learned that their cooking oil is highly flammable and burns and evaporates quickly.

You will not encounter fear and doubt when you are receptive to the noble heart, and bliss occupies your mind completely. There will be no room for confusing thoughts. In such a state of bliss, you can realize that all miserable situations that arise from confusing thoughts cannot distract you from your true happiness. Many find themselves in this state and lead blissful lives. It is not as rare as you might think. I hope you are already there or getting closer to it.

However, you may think happiness is satisfying and that it is also a fleeting phenomenon. Such thought processes are also the doing of your fictional character. It would be best to recognize that satisfaction and happiness are opposite sides of a coin. Satisfaction stems from the mind, and happiness stems from the noble heart. When the mind dominates, we do not enjoy our true self. When inner peace is prominent, we distance ourselves from our self-images to experience the bliss of being alive—the *true self.* If you think bliss is "satisfying," your mind dominates to obscure the amazing benefits of being alive. I encourage you to cultivate your interest in inner peace and sustain your blissful sensations. Once you recognize and sustain the blissful sensations in you and realize the benefits, the interest to dwell in your true self is inevitable.

Going beyond our fictional character is like needing to go outside in order to be able to see the entire house. We cannot see its entirety when we are inside the house, the fictional character. Once we step outside of our minds, we see the miseries in us as a trick of our minds, and we can take our attention away from those miseries. Use your experience from any practice you have done so far to move attention to inner peace. Your miseries will fade away, and this will open your heart and direct you to blissful sensations. You cannot conceptualize and interpret bliss or true happiness; you must experience it firsthand. Therefore, recognize your bliss through our practices and sustain it as long as you can.

Thoughts or perceptions are absent when you are in a moment of bliss or being happy. Therefore, happiness is not what you get from someone or something; it is what you experience. The closer you are to recognizing bliss, the greater your chances of being happy and at peace with your true self. As mentioned earlier, there are times when you feel you've done enough thinking and need to get away by going to a park or taking a vacation. This urge stems from your longing for inner peace. In other words, you're longing for a quiet moment—true happiness—from your true self. Underlying this thirst for complete mental relaxation is the stirrings of the noble heart.

Let's return to Aristotle, a student of Plato in ancient Athens. His philosophy uniquely influenced almost every form of knowledge in the West. Once again, in my assessment, Aristotle was also a great philosopher who became a sage. He was a seeker of wisdom who later became a bearer of wisdom. He confirmed this by his statement, "Happiness depends upon ourselves." This means he recognized that happiness is not something we get from outside or by conceptualizing, and we need to experience happiness within ourselves when it sprouts from our noble hearts.

If you think you are happy, that is again the steering of your mind. You cannot think about happiness; you need to experience it, which is why it exists beyond your self-image. True happiness is the inner peace that we share with nature. We will further explore our true self and inner peace in the next chapter.

Inner Peace

I trust that you now know to what extent you have inner peace. While reading this, you may have improved your receptivity to your noble heart. Or you may feel you are at a certain point between the noble heart and the enslaved mind. In other words, between the extreme approach of sage or philosopher. These extremes are like the ends of a balanced scale; if you lean toward either edge, it will tilt to that side. Likewise, if you cherish either of the approaches, eventually, you will tilt toward becoming either a great philosopher or a great sage. You will fall into the ocean of inner peace from the edge of that extreme. It will help if you are determined to walk to any edge of your approach to find your noble heart and fall into the ocean of inner peace. Either way, happiness is the path to your inner peace. Therefore, now you have to let go of the image of the philosopher or sage and focus on pleasantness or the bliss within you.

Here, we go deeper than you have learned so far through reading and practicing. I trust that you can feel pleasantness in yourself after the practices you have done till now. We want to extend that pleasantness further to dwell in inner peace. For that, you need to recognize the innermost obstacles to your inner peace at this stage.

Self-check

When you are ill, you take a step back from the daily rat race and pause and relax. At that time, you have more time to look inward and explore within. You notice every bodily pain and agitation. All body aches and conditions of the illness take you to reality. You break away from your self-image to focus on your longing for peace and well-being. Once you fully recover from your illness, you feel your longing is satisfied. This longing is the rudimentary search for happiness. You do not have to seek or get it from outside. Instead, move your attention to inner peace and experience true happiness. Then you can be happy at war or in the middle of a pandemic.

You are on the brink of that transformation. Sometimes you may feel inner peace, yet minuscule unhappiness is still in your heart. This is because, at a deeper level, you seek perceived worldly satisfaction.

True happiness is not only living without stress and problems but also living without doubt and fear, which is achieved by dwelling in inner peace. We need to learn how to eliminate the friction inside us to surge the bliss through our noble hearts. This rudimentary level of mental friction is regret about imperfection.

Have you noticed that regretful thoughts create friction in you? You cannot change anything that happened in the past, but you are still worried about it. Many regrets are based on others' opinions, or on that-did-or-did-not-happen scenarios. None of these can be reversed now. Yet your mind ponders on them to take you to misery. Consequently, anxiety, depression, and regrets are illnesses created by your mind. I invite you to check yourself, investigate this fact, forgive yourself for what you have done in the past, and heal your lifelong illness.

You can do this by focusing on the present and current situation and forgiving. Your regrets and worries will disappear when you forgive yourself, and you will experience true happiness. As Buddha said, "happiness is the path"; we travel this path, stage by stage, by being happy at different levels.

I do not regret my past. Hence, I am free from inner friction. Please forgive your past and be free from stress, depression, and worries. You will distance yourself from your nagging mind and live blissfully. I trust that you are already experiencing this. If not, practice the following.

Practice # 13: Experiencing True Happiness
When you move attention to inner peace, you experience true happiness.

Contemplate the relief you get after recovering from the flu or any illness that lasted a few days. All your body aches are gone, your mind is clear from all worries, and what a pleasant feeling it is! Focus on that pleasantness surging in you right now. Let that soothing feeling of well-being rise to your head. Please pay attention to that bubble of joy, and let it expand and spread beyond your physical body. Stay with that feeling even if your attention is outside your body. You will feel free from all sensory perceptions, as if you were on a weightless cloud. Your body is there but without any associated agitation. You are in supreme relaxation. What you are experiencing is true happiness—*inner peace*—at a deeper level.

Inner peace is the base of our lives, like the ocean floor is the base of the ocean. We may ignore this with our thoughts, perceptions, and emotions; they are like the ocean's waves, tides, and undercurrents. You just moved your attention from such delusions to your inner peace, like diving down to touch the ocean floor. You will sense that you live distantly from your body and mind. When your attention is fully vested in inner peace, you experience your core being away from your body and mind. Hence, you experience the bliss of being alive at a much deeper level!

When I contemplate the phrase "the bliss of being alive," my attention instantly sinks deeper, and inner silence surges through me to such a degree that I hear my heartbeat. The longer I stay in that state, the more intense the silence becomes, and inner peace emerges with true happiness. I live a bit away from my mind and body, and my body may ache, but I do not suffer from it. I respond to everything with inner peace, without agitation or mental friction. You could do the same when you practice this and experience inner peace at the deepest level.

If you pursue happiness, you chase it without experiencing it, like sailing on the ocean. Instead, we need to detect peace and cherish our happiness in every moment, like jumping into the water and diving down to find the ocean floor. One of the obstacles to this is the sense of satisfaction created by our fictional character. We find satisfaction in our money, house, or appearance, natural or with makeup that will last only a few hours. A new concept of happiness comes to our mind to obstruct that satisfaction. However, when we usher in our bliss, this obstacle will fade away, and the nobility of our hearts will open up for us. Once you make this a habit, you will be at peace. Hence there will be no stress, problems, doubt, or fear in your life. With such an approach, you can return to the state of bliss you were born with and experience the bliss of being alive. My attempt here is to help you get to that state of living, and I hope you are almost there, if not already experiencing it.

You must have noticed that we talked about the mind and the heart as two separate faculties. One could even say that they are not faculties but representatives of two types of approaches: a philosopher and a sage. The common philosopher challenges all ideas and chases satisfaction or seeks a fleeting sense of happiness through their mind. Philosophers mostly dwell in their minds and, occasionally, recognize their hearts.

Sages, on the contrary, live in their hearts, with little room in their minds for satisfaction or disappointment. They accept the prevailing conditions around them and try to adapt themselves accordingly. Yet their minds can potentially cheat them of that ideal state of being and create perceptions and streams of thought that can rob their inner peace unless they are great sages.

I would like you to explore memories from your past and see whether you can enhance your inner peace. In your journey through life, you have probably asked yourself the following questions: Who am I? Why was I born? What am I doing on this planet? My experience tells me that there are two inherited cognitive fields—*intuitions*—behind those questions. As a self-check for you, we will explore those intuitions one by one.

Self-check

Here is the first type of intuition: Have you ever pondered that the universe has a common structure or pattern? In fact, the day you grasped the principle underlying the system of planets revolving around the sun, perhaps your instinct told you that this principle applies to everything around you. Think of the discovery that every atom operates on similar principles, with electrons moving around the nucleus. Now, consider that every single cell around you also operates under the same principle. Would that idea increase the fascination dormant in you all along, from birth? If you follow your instinct, you will discover that everything around you follows the same fundamental principle. Perhaps you would like to be in harmony with nature to experience the comfort in life? You could, in fact, be reading this book to discover the answers to the curiosity that besets you. Sound familiar? It's the seed of a sage you inherited despite approaching life like a philosopher.

If that is not the case, you have the other type of intuition. Your experiences may have taught you that there is more than what meets the eye. Your faith or compulsions may have led you to believe that there is a divine force behind everything in this world. You may have been seeking satisfaction from the outside world like a philosopher; nevertheless, your inner experience was probably deep enough to convince you that a God or universal intelligence governs everything. Although you think that you are more of a philosopher, this is the quality of the sage surging in you. In other words, both intuitions come from one source.

If you continue your quest, you will come to the same realization; whether it is based on instinct or faith, you will recognize that there is a common principle governing the whole world. This is in every human being from birth, and gradually leads them to evolve and recognize their inner peace. Therefore, whether you are a philosopher or a sage, your noble heart shares a common ground with this universal principle. If we go back to the analogy of the sketch of a face once more, its white surface represents the universal principle of inner peace. When interpreting the drawing on it, we build our self-image in black ink. Philosophers start from the image drawn with black ink and later notice the white background that gives birth to it. On the other hand, sages see the white background with clarity and then notice the black ink forming an image on the surface. To experience true happiness, both need pure attention to space between the thoughts and let inner peace blossom.

As I mentioned, self-image surfaces in your mind by creating perceptions and concepts, just as black ink forms an image on white paper. Inner peace is an image-free phenomenon in your heart, like pristine white paper without marks or images. The answer to the questions "Who am I?" or "What is my true self?" is inner peace! However, you may think otherwise, depending on the predominance of your cloud of perceptions. In other words, your self-image and the degree to which the black ink covers the white surface—*your true self*—gives you a different answer to those questions. As long as you conceptualize yourself, and think that you are a person or an "I," then your self-image will persist. Once the conceptualization ceases, you experience "us," our true selves—*inner peace*.

The great philosophers of this world, unhindered by limitations and unbiased by perceptions, recognize the nature of the heart buried deep within. In order to achieve greatness and enjoy a blissful life, a philosopher needs to explore matters inwardly and examine every aspect of their questions. This dissolves the self-image created by the mind. Then the noble heart—*our true self*—that we were born with will surface.

As a philosopher, you have to look inwardly to experience inner peace. All your questioning should be directed toward inner feelings. Investigate, and identify whether your interaction creates mental friction. If so, let go of such physical, oral, or emotional interaction and move your attention to inner peace. For that, you could use one of the practices I have introduced here. Once you settle in your true self, you can instantly respond efficiently to anything that comes your way.

If you are a sage, you should often recognize the noble nature of your heart—*your true self*. You may be experiencing bliss and inner peace intermittently. But if you are a great sage, you will never become a victim of your mind because you recognize the inner peace every second of your life and you will be at peace with yourself forever—*dwelling in that inner peace*. Then, you will interact outwardly with no interruption to your true self. First, you must find true happiness for at least a fraction of a second, using one of the practices I introduced. Then the foundation of inner peace gets established. After that, inner peace becomes a strong underlying quality, and it surges upwardly within you to keep you blissful all the time. Now, you have become a different kind of person, acting effortlessly from a place of pure attention. I like to illustrate this upward phenomenon as follows:

Pure attention /Awareness

Noble Heart / Blissfulness

Inner Peace / True Happiness / True self

Once you clear your thoughts and turn inwards toward your inner peace and dwell in it clear of any agitations, the surge of the above upward phenomenon is inevitable. Therefore, there won't be mental friction in your daily life, and you can interact with the outside world while dwelling in your true self. Your inner peace works outwardly through your noble heart with pure attention to resolve any situation.

I trust that I have enhanced your enthusiasm for such blissful living. Some of the techniques in this book are provided to bring about that enthusiasm. Practicing these techniques will assist you in diving deeper into inner peace. Once you see the benefits, you might be encouraged to continue practicing. Then you can live blissfully and respond with inner peace rather than reacting to any situation.

With that skill, you can rapidly reach inner peace by using a phrase like "the bliss of being alive" or "worldly satisfaction obscures true happiness" or any of the phrases I use as the leading quote for each practice in this book.

When you totally recognize your true self, other activities and situations are little waves in the outer ring of the lake hitting the shore. Like deep water in the lake, you are still, peaceful, and free of doubt and fear. You will still live through your body and mind, while experiencing the bliss of being alive—*true happiness.*

A person who spontaneously jumps into a raging stream of water to rescue a stranger interrupts the myriad thoughts in their head with pure attention, overcoming fear and doubt instantly, with intuitive courage surging from the noble heart, acting on the heart's guidance without the mind's interference. You have already developed that level of spiritual courage, which I call an upward phenomenon. I trust that you can now dwell in inner peace directly by recognizing and distancing from your confusing thoughts in every situation.

After trying those practices so far, if your logical mind still obstructs your happiness, you may not have experienced true happiness. Here, I share another practice designed to enable you to follow bliss, distance yourself from the self-image, and be free from misery.

Practice # 14: Embracing the Dawn
Embracing the calmness in the dawn
gives you a brighter day.

Start your day by paying attention and embracing the calmness in the dawn. First, take a deep breath and hold it as long as possible. Then let it go, experiencing the relief and relaxation running through your body as you exhale. Stay in that space for a few minutes. Now focus on silence and stillness in your surroundings. Then let your attention spread into the freshness and calmness of the dawn. Embrace that calmness and freshness with your heart. You will notice peaceful and blissful sensations emerge through that silent moment. Fathom this experience and silence for a few minutes until it sinks into your core.

During the rest of the day, recall that peaceful and blissful moment frequently. You will feel calm within. With that base, you will see where your attention is. Is it creating frictions, seeking satisfaction, or are you content with bliss? After a few days, it will become second nature to you. You will see the consequences or drawbacks of confusing thoughts. They cling to perceptions and create friction with others or make situations challenging. Once you experience true happiness firsthand, you will be convinced that such thoughts interrupt your happiness. This will be engrained in your heart and pop up frequently, like a song stuck in your head. Once you experience such convincing proof of happiness, peaceful living is inevitable! Are you experiencing the bliss of being alive now? I am.

Try the above practice daily to sustain this bliss throughout the day. This enables you to respond to each situation rather than react to it and will empower you to be happy in all circumstances. This true happiness is permanent and persists even during times of chaos. When you are experiencing inner peace, every incident is another occurrence in the present moment. It did not happen in the past and will not happen in the fearful future. Therefore, you live with it happily. You have no choice, yet the mind may think otherwise.

With your experiments so far, you have had a firsthand experience of true happiness, irrespective of your approach to life. To sustain it, experience the following practice. If you do this properly, I assure you that you will want to repeat it frequently until you dwell in inner peace permanently.

Practice # 15: Experiencing Inner Peace
The deeper level of inner peace brings equanimity.
You need to spend at least 20 to 60 minutes with this practice at the start to get the expected benefits; this time can differ from person to person. In addition, it may depend on your

age. Spend one minute for each year of your age. For example, if you are 20 years old, spend 20 minutes, and one hour if you are 60. This time frame is needed only at the beginning. Once you experience the depth of inner peace, you will not need much time to dive into it again.

Find a quiet place to do this practice. Sit comfortably, keep your back straight, and relax your body as much as you can. Take a deep breath and exhale without effort while relaxing your entire body. Your attention should travel from forehead to toe, relaxing your body. Do this a couple more times and relax for a few minutes between each attempt. Next, breathe effortlessly; do not take deep breaths anymore; just notice your breathing. Follow the air coming in with a soothing sensation through your nostrils and into the lungs. Sensing this air movement through your body will relax your mind, and pure attention will surge within you. With your exhale, relax your body as you did during the first few deep breaths. Let this effortless breathing and relaxation calm your mind and body until you feel lighter and free from thoughts. Effortlessly, your eyes should be half or fully closed once you completely relax your body and mind. A slight smile will appear with a glimpse of bliss.

Now fully relaxed, gradually bring your attention to the silence and stillness above your head. Recognize the pleasantness stemming from that and dwell there. After a few minutes, you will feel that pleasantness intensifying and spreading through your surroundings. Please stay in this state as long as you can. Eventually, your attention will settle on the luminous pleasantness above your head. You will feel tranquility, free from agitation and tightness in your mind and body. At this stage, breathing would be like a bird's chirp or the clicking sound of a clock you hear from a distance in the thick silence. In addition, your heartbeat could be like noise from an external source.

Spend some time allowing this condition to mature within and without!

You will notice intensifying silence and luminous pleasantness in you. Follow it as it spreads through you to the surrounding space like an expanding ring or pattern. You do not have to think or make an effort, but keep your attention focused on this phenomenon as long as you can. You will feel similar rings of pleasantness appear and disappear within you, and you will experience inner peace at its best. If you do this correctly, you will be naturally drawn into your noble heart and encouraged to stay there until you go beyond your mind to dwell in inner peace permanently, bringing serenity to you and the world.

In this serenity, you, me, and everyone are the same, and we are in the same reservoir of inner peace. You will not react to anything or anyone as you see your deeper level in others and respond to everyone and any situation equally and effectively with equanimity.

The Buddha, who examined the mind through his teachings, puts the greatest emphasis on people finding equanimity in the experience of living rather than achieving happiness at a later date. He said, "There is no path to happiness; happiness is the path," indicating that there is no goal; awakening is here and now. You can make your happiness by awakening now, not at the end of life's journey or the next birth. The Buddha taught others how to purify the mind and distance themselves from mind-created suffering to be happy in the present. He taught that this can be achieved by recognizing the cause of suffering: the mind-made miseries. In other words, he taught us how to become a bearer of wisdom rather than one seeking it. So, irrespective of your approach, you can find the nobility of your heart—*your true self*—to experience the bliss of being alive—*true happiness*!

You can easily liberate yourself from your self-image when you identify your true self. You should not be fixated on any self-image that will limit your true happiness. Eventually, you must also release the self-image of a philosopher or sage to embrace your true self. It would be best if you learned to dwell in inner peace, free of any concept, which is what you feel when you can go beyond your self-image.

There are many teachings to take you there by clearing your path through the jungle of thoughts and concepts, to access pure attention and dive deep into the noble heart and dwell in inner peace. We will discuss those in the final part of the book.

Part IV

How to Experience
Our True Selves?

Ancient Path

By now, you must have experienced your true self, at least to some extent. From ancient times to this day, many methods have been used for this purpose, and such methods are taught in our spiritual doctrines, social ethics, and other peace-loving teachings. I'll connect the dots with my experience to help you discover the path to inner peace in your faith. When I looked at my true story, I realized I had followed this ancient path throughout my life. Especially when I explore inwardly, I have seen that diving into inner peace is the path many spiritual teachers have taught.

In my research, I found that various methods and approaches are necessary to cater to people with different temperaments and self-images. That is why different people find themselves drawn to different religions and teachings. I have noticed that the rudimentary process of dwelling in inner peace, referred to as the ancient path in many religious teachings, is the only path to go beyond self-image. I like it very much because it brings a common ground to all faiths. However, this path is presented differently at the surface level to attract followers with varied perceptions. Once you investigate deeper, though, it all comes down to elevating pure attention to our noble heart and then to inner peace, which is the method I have presented throughout this book. This method is the direct or ancient path in many spiritual teachings.

I learned that the Hebrew word for *ancient* is *Olam*. Olam means old, concealed, hidden, perpetual, eternal, timeless, and from eternity. I like all those meanings since this path is old, concealed, and hidden from our fictional characters. It came from eternity and is timeless and perpetual, so the ancient path is used throughout all civilizations from ancient to modern day.

You were on this path even before reading this book. As mentioned earlier, my effort is to assist you in clearing your pathway and accelerating the process you have naturally been following with these new practices. You can benefit from them and share that profound experience with many others. Keep doing the relevant self-checks and practices throughout this book that resonate with you. Most importantly, pay attention to the blissful sensation kindled in you throughout this journey and beyond, and that will provide the necessary encouragement and conditions to connect with your faith and inner peace.

Rupert Spira, born in 1960, is another modern-day sage who shares his true self with the public as a spiritual teacher and writer. He teaches the "direct path," a method of spiritual self-inquiry through experiencing awareness. In my view, this "direct path" is synonymous with the ancient path used in other spiritual teachings.

In one of his discussions, posted on December 11, 2020, on YouTube, titled *Nondual Consciousness: A Dialogue between Rupert Spira and Swami Sarvapriyananda,* he clearly articulates popular religion's inward and outward approaches that imply the same outcome.

The inward approach is a self-inquiry method used by most nondualist religions, and the outward approach is faith and devotion-based dualistic religions. I see that these approaches resemble the qualities of sages and philosophers, respectively. Therefore, you do not need to change your religion or approach to experience your true self—true happiness. Once you identify your approach to life and settle in your true self, you will see the relevance of such a doctrine with clarity. You will see all religions directing their followers toward true happiness. You will realize that you do not need to discriminate against any group of people or individuals. We all seek the same happiness and will experience the same in the universal reservoir of inner peace. That will be the day we all celebrate world peace in the true sense.

Your aim may be self-realization, and someone else's may be a union with God or vice versa. You regret that others are not on the right path and build friction with them in your mind, or you are clinging to your faith so completely that you reject others. As we discussed, this is your mistake, not theirs. If this friction or clinging is still in you, I hope the following self-check may help.

Self-check

As mentioned earlier, you should know that any regretful thoughts create friction in you. You cannot change anything that happened in the past, so why are you worrying about it?

Anxiety, depression, and regrets are illnesses created by our minds. Instead, focus on the current situation, available right here and now. Experience the practices in this book and bring your attention to inner peace. You will find that at least one of the practices gives you the experience of inner peace. Use the practice that resonates with you to experience inner peace instantly. Your regrets and worries will disappear, and you will experience true happiness. Your bodily pains are another thought and perception. You will feel your pain but you will not suffer since it occurs outside your inner peace.

I recently learned that Moses is one of the personalities recognized by many as the messenger of God. I understand that he is one of the most important prophets in Christianity, Islam, the Druze faith, the Baháí faith, and many other Abrahamic religions. While the possibility of Moses or a Moses-like figure existed in the 13th century BCE, sometimes Moses is seen as a legendary figure. I consider he transcended from self-image to true self and helped many people, irrespective of their faith.

Many personalities such as Moses exist in Eastern religions and cultures. There are many stories around them, and they helped many, irrespective of their faith. They are prominent figures who have mystic powers, according to legend. They are like Moses, who transcended from self-image to true self. In Vedic tradition, the Buddha is one of the avatars of the god Shiva. Many myths and stories are interpretations of others, but these great personalities' true selves are quite different from those of fictional characters. Einstein also saw this and wrote in his September 1937 letter about Buddha, Moses, and Jesus: "what these blessed men have given us we must guard and try to keep alive with all our strength if humanity is not to lose its dignity, the security of its existence, and its joy in living."

Therefore, I would like you to clear your perception of other religions and focus on the similarities between your faith and others. It could be something common such as believing in God when your God is different from theirs. My favorite common feature is the massive space inside the church, mosque, temple, or synagogue, irrespective of the architecture or outside appearance. That grandiose space gives you the feeling of pure attention when you are inside that building, and it gets you closer to your inner peace, promoted by all faith and spiritual teachings. That space is within you, and your pure attention is the church in you, and it gives you access to it without even going to your place of worship.

You can eliminate reactions to mind-made emotions of other faiths by eliminating friction and not clinging to your faith. When you practice your faith by discriminating against other faiths, you are clinging to it. Once you let go of it, you can match the experiences by which great philosophers and sages have lived. You have already discovered whether you can do so and how receptive you are to your noble heart. Once you eliminate friction and clinging, you will enjoy inner peace. Then you will respond to any situation like a great sage, without making it a problem or a stressful event.

I would like you to practice the following to experience friction-free living, especially with people who follow a faith other than yours.

Practice # 16: Eliminating Friction
Mental friction or aversion is your flaw and not someone else's fault.

As a sage, you may be quick to read someone's facial expression. You may instantly run through your thought process when you see someone making a face, following something you did or said, leading you to judge and react. It may turn into arguments and quarrels. This is, again, friction, a flaw in you. Making a face may have happened intentionally or unintentionally, purposely or out of habit, and that person may regret the unintentional reaction. Still, you might react, verbalize, and get into a quarrel with that person. In that case, friction or aversion is a flaw in you and not in the other person. So, be attentive to all your reactions, identify them as your flaws, and correct them then and there. You will recognize the ease and sense of bliss surging through you when friction is absent. Once you master this, you can take your attention away from the pain of a needle prick and smile at the nurse. Or you will be able to compassionately look and smile at a mosquito drawing your blood to satisfy its hunger.

Pause for a moment and contemplate forgiving yourself and every person and incident bothering you. Let go of all thoughts and perceptions built upon those things and free your mind. Forgiving is not cowardice; it is a divine quality you carried from birth. Forgiving clears your cluttered mind and frees it for pure attention, a much better use.

You can use this technique at home or work to resolve any friction or conflicts. You are cultivating a very good soft skill that helps your personality and, best of all, your receptivity to your true self.

Although there are many accounts of Moses in the Bible, Quran, and other scriptures, one story of him stands out to me. A story in one of the best-known passages from the Bible: Moses parts the Red Sea so that his people can cross on their journey to the promised land. According to historians, this story of the Hebrew's exodus from Egypt is found in the first five books of the Bible and in the Quran. No other ancient sources corroborate the story, and no archaeological evidence supports it. This has led many scholars to conclude that Moses was a legendary figure and the exodus story a cultural myth.

Nevertheless, my intuition tells me that this parable resembles the Buddhist simile about the first stage of awakening. One who realizes the non-self sees it as the bottom of a body of water, and it is visible when the water is parted by the force of a fallen tree trunk. This opening leads to the noble eightfold path— Buddha's Ancient path to awakening. I notice that a similar path is described in Hinduism as Ashtanga yoga, which will lead a practitioner to union or *Vimukthi*—freedom. Further, Jeremiah the prophet instructed the people of Jerusalem about the path they ought to follow: "Stand by in the ways and see and ask for the ancient paths, where the good way is, and walk in it; and you will find rest for your souls." (Jeremiah 6:16).

Therefore, I believe that Eastern philosophies and religions, as well as Western Abrahamic religions, and others, direct their followers to a self-realization of oneness—inner peace. The ancient path is not physical, historical, or legendary; it is the path everyone should take to find their true self. The story of the Hebrew's exodus from Egypt is a mythical representation of how Moses led people to the promised land of inner peace. That makes me conclude that all religions and spiritual teachings, one way or another, promote the universal truth of inner peace, which is true happiness.

Many modern-day spiritual teachers emphasize living in the present moment. I realized that in order to get to the present, we need to distance ourselves from our fictional characters. I followed ancient teachings, parted the mind-created sea of confusion and doubts, and walked on that ancient path to inner peace that I am sharing with you now. Most ancient teachings try to bring tranquility in grand cathedral-like structures or repeated prayer. This approach is designed to distance your mind from your awareness and enable you to experience tranquility in the present moment. In other words, it is designed to elevate pure attention and open the ancient path for you. This experience refers to being with God, oneness, liberation, and enlightenment. Certain teachings take a philosophical approach and scrutinize our minds deeply, to pixel level, to help us distance ourselves from the mind and enable us to live in the present.

These different pathways are the water flowing through streams into one river, ending in the ocean of inner peace. Therefore, it is not that one religion becomes the global religion; instead, all humans will recognize that the doctrine of every religion is directing us to the same wisdom, truth, true happiness, or inner peace.

You may have read various books on this subject, and many may have directed you to live in the present. When you are contemplating or conceptualizing the present, you do it within your enslaved mind's limitations. You may suppress thinking about the past and future but still think about the present moment, which is a conceptualized moment. To live in the present, you need to go beyond conceptual limitations. That is why you need to distance yourself from your mind and mind-made discriminations. The practices I introduce take your attention directly to experience true happiness in the present moment, beyond the conceptual "Now." Therefore, you dwell in inner peace and transcend to your true self rather than thinking about or contemplating it.

The practices in this book show you how to transcend your true self, layer by layer, as illustrated below.

Pure Attention

Noble Heart

Inner Peace / True Self

The first layer of transcendence happens when you identify your pure attention, free of thoughts and perceptions. This level of awareness is commonly practiced in the corporate world to achieve profits and global expansion. Modern-day motivational speakers promote awareness as a tool to achieve personal and corporate goals. I see this as clearing the first layer of obstacles to inner peace. With this level of pure attention, you may perceive high satisfaction. As we defined in an earlier chapter, this satisfaction will last until your next perception of satisfaction is formed.

Once people realize the changing nature of these conditions, they become depressed and seek inner happiness. If you are one of them, you now know how to dive deep into your heart with the experiences you had from the practices you did earlier. Especially when you unleash your identities and discriminations and become free from mental friction. Then, you fall into the noble heart, which is blissful and free of discrimination. Once you dwell in your noble heart, you develop empathy and care for others. However, this is also with the help of your self-image at a subtler level. If I may use an analogy, it is as if you peeled most of the layers from your self-image, but a few inner layers remained in the onion of your self-image.

Once you let go of that innermost notion of self, you will fall into the reservoir of inner peace, which is free from mental clinging and friction. You may still be on the brink of this transcendence, and we will further dive into this in the following chapters.

When you investigate deeper, you will see your faith or religion has a sector that focuses on spiritual practices rather than worshiping, rituals, or praying. They may be practiced by priests, hermits, or leaders of the order, and they are more devoted to the practices, since their commitment is greater than their followers. At that level, they adhere to similar practices as the ancient path, irrespective of differences in their various traditions that they exhibit to the outer world. They go through the same process I described above and eventually dwell in inner peace.

This ancient path is the process of transcendence to our true selves that I present throughout this book and will elaborate on in the next chapter.

Transcendence

As with the ancient simile of change in a tadpole's life cycle to a frog, we need to transcend from self-image to our true selves to experience true happiness. This happens when we excel in pure attention to a deeper experience of blissfulness and then dwell in inner peace. This transcending is the core teaching in all peace-loving religions, faiths, and spiritual doctrines. However, many followers of those teachings try to conceptualize this process and hang on the brink of transcendence, unable to get the benefit, sometimes doubting their own faith.

When you let go of your identity, you have cleared the pathway, like you do when walking in the woods by cutting shrubs and tree branches that block your path. When your mind is clear of discriminating thoughts and perceptions, you have the pure attention to go beyond your self-image. Your noble heart and inner peace unravel effortlessly once your pure attention excels and is persistent in you. That helps you transcend to inner peace, your true self. You cannot think and forcefully get it, but it will happen when you are persistent in your pure attention.

If you are in the present with pure attention, intensified bliss—*inner peace*—will inevitably bloom in you, and then you will realize that it is your true self. Many modern-day spiritual teachings successfully bring to the surface the true self and refer to it as being in the present—*the Now*. The Now is promoted as wisdom, as a rudimentary doctrine in most ancient spiritual teachings as well. However, only a few skillful humans live in the present, bearing true wisdom. Often, many followers of great teachers live in a conceptual Now.

As we discussed, if you take the philosopher's approach, you first need to eliminate identification with your self-image. This includes all discriminatory identities, such as nationality, race, and gender. This will give you the freedom to interact with other people without friction. You can draw calmness from nature and experience inner peace by being still and silent. Then you will have a clear mind and be able to listen to any ideas with an open heart. This empowers you to respond calmly to any situation. You will respond to all situations, like nature's reflection on calm water. You will not react with preconceived ideas but will respond effectively.

In fact, reaction stems from our deep-rooted perceptions. We react to frightening sounds with our survival instincts, built into our DNA as a defense mechanism through our evolutionary processes. Our enslaved minds then elevate this survival tool to react to everything to protect our self-images. That is taking our survival techniques too far. In the extreme, this can lead to mass-scale fighting and killing. Based on your perceptions, you fight and kill with your emotions in your self-image at the micro-level. Once you dwell in inner peace, this microlevel reaction will not happen, just as you cannot draw a line on the water; you will not react to any situation but will respond wisely.

Amongst many incidents, I'll share one to demonstrate this condition of inner peace with you. One participant tested me in one of the group sittings by dropping a heavy object close to me, making a loud noise. Since I was in deep meditation, dwelling in inner peace, I noticed it as a little vibration in a distant location; it did not shake me one bit. But some of the other people panicked and ran around, learning later that it was a surprise test performed on me by someone who doubted my practice and the experience of inner peace I had been sharing with them.

Transcendence will occur when you excel in pure attention, which you may have experienced during one of the practices

I introduced here. As I said earlier, it is not a conceptualized state of mind. You will be drawn into inner peace when you keep pure attention to your noble heart. So it is not what you think or contemplate, but an experience you have. When this transcendence happens, you will recognize this world differently, like a frog sees water differently than a tadpole sees it.

Like the frog, nature provides another example of transcendence with the butterfly. A butterfly's life cycle is amazing; watching it is so much fun. Butterflies have four life stages: the egg, the caterpillar or larva, the pupa or chrysalis, and the adult butterfly. It is like a philosopher's gradual transcendence in becoming a great sage. Philosophers first must understand their approach clearly, then cultivate pure attention to identify the noble heart, which leads to dwelling in their true selves, and then to the experience of true happiness, just as a fully grown butterfly flies away freely. I can easily connect those four stages to the four awakening stages in Buddha's teachings. These stages are: stream-winner, once-returner, non-returner, and fully awakened one. In his teachings, Buddha provided us with inward and outward approaches to awakening. I see similar approaches in other spiritual teachings, too.

I trust that you are reading this book to satisfy yourself or bring peace to your mind by discovering your true self. Please do not consider that reading this text will merely satisfy you or give you a fleeting moment of bliss. I presented our dialogues in different dimensions to avoid such considerations and help you to experience true happiness firsthand. The techniques I use, such as repetition, avoiding common words, and providing experiential anecdotes, are used for your benefit. I trust I have succeeded in my efforts. I am revealing this now rather than in my introduction because learning this beforehand would have hindered your experience.

Whatever the case, I urge you to go deeper and recognize your true self. That is what you are truly looking for as you read this book, and every word here aims to reward you with that very thing. I might have failed to override your preconceived perceptions. If that is the case, please follow some modern-day spiritual teachers I've mentioned to get more help, or revisit the practices with the help of the index provided at the end of this text.

Your true self empowers you to respond to any situation and be happy in all circumstances. You will recognize that all situations are like nature's reflection in calm water or a bird's chirp in the stillness of dawn. Just as this can calm your mind, it can make an impression of true happiness on your heart.

Once you have such an impression of happiness, you will never be victim to your mind-initiated problems or satisfactions. You will be happy without lapses.

Self-check

It may be that you do not have this level of experience. You may notice some agitation—*friction or rejection, even desires or that you still cling to something*—disturbing your inner peace. It is a sign of the practices you have done, working to some extent. Your heart is tuned to identify such minute vibrations within you. You see someone or some incident like the drawing of a line on the sandy beach of your noble heart. Once you identify that, you should be skillful in wiping that line off and returning to your true self. In other words, when you notice something bothering you, you should be able to move your attention back to your true self and let go of the disturbance with little effort. A wave of bliss could wash off that line drawn on the sandy shore of your noble heart, pull it into the ocean of inner peace. With that, you should be able to respond to a situation rather than react to it. If someone said something to make you angry, you would notice anger arising in you, but you should be able to let go of it and return to inner peace. Then you will respond to the situation instead of reacting.

When you have this ability, you will be delighted to see how much your inner peace is helping your life. I have met many people who enjoy life in this way. However, my true happiness experience is much deeper than this. As I described earlier, it is free from any mental clinging or friction. If you repeat the following practice a few times, I am confident that you will transcend to inner peace and become like water, where no one and nothing can draw a line on your heart or make you agitated. That is the experience of true happiness at the deepest level, establishing unwavering inner peace in you.

Practice # 17: Letting Go
Letting go of inner friction and clinging brings lasting happiness.

Your vow should ensure that each event in your life is free from friction and clinging. Be alert and identify the agitation—good or bad—that comes with your interaction with others or your thoughts and emotions. Such agitation could be aversion—friction—to that event or your desire to have something or someone, and with such thirst that you cling to it. Your friction and clinging happen at a deeper level, which is very subtle. With the help of the practices in this book, you can recognize and let go of such subtle events within you. When you let go of them, you will calm your mind, and instead of reacting to any situation, you will respond to it.

Once you improve on those practices, navigate your attention to the noise around you. Then take your attention off the outside noise and direct it toward the buzzing noise inside. Perhaps you have never noticed this cosmic buzzing noise before. If you have effectively completed at least one of the practices mentioned throughout this book, with your pure attention, you will recognize a subtle cosmic noise on one side of your head and a supreme silence on the other side. Dwell in that supreme silence to experience clinging and friction-free inner peace — true happiness. You will begin to experience intense inner peace. Your habit of letting go will become a cognitive reality. Like a line cannot be drawn on water, nothing will disturb your inner peace in that supreme silence. You will transcend to your true self and dwell in inner peace. Then you will respond to all situations effortlessly.

You will live beyond the concept of the present moment and a slight ways away from your mind and body.

Once you have succeeded, you can experience the life of a great philosopher and sage. You have already discovered whether you can do so and how far you are along that path. Explore the noble heart within you further and dive deep into the depths of universal inner peace, for this is something you alone can do for yourself; no one else can do it on your behalf. Do not be a victim of external stimuli and others' opinions. Distance yourself from your fictional character and begin to enjoy your true self — *inner peace.*

Wisdom

I hope this experiential journey has helped you discover who you are, opening your heart to inner peace. With that, you notice your true self and the fictional character you have been living with all along. Our primary objective was to explore the depths of your heart and the peace that resides within you, which is your true self. In other words, this exploration allows you to recognize life as it is, get closer to your true self, and live a bit away from your mind and body. The greater the peace in you, the better you can recognize the bliss within your heart and in others. The closer you get to your noble heart, the more you will be blissful while enjoying health and peace of mind in this challenging world. That is your wisdom. When you dwell in inner peace, you bear wisdom!

In summary, when you pause and focus on something, you will see it entirely for a fraction of a second, free of perceptions. Your instinct is at work, and your heart is involved. It is a state of blissfulness. Your mind does not take precedence in this experience; your mind no longer controls you. If you sustain such attention—*pure attention*—you have access to your noble heart and eventually dwell in inner peace. With such unwavering inner peace, you will be able to accept situations as they are, wisely adapting and using them to better yourself and others. That is intelligent decision-making—*wisdom*.

You will interact with every person in your life in harmony. This might be called a "soft skill" that you can use at work, home, and in any other challenging situation. You will effortlessly respond to situations with wisdom and not react to others' omissions and commissions. You will become a bearer of wisdom!

Wisdom is what you get through your experience rather than conceptualizing or studying. Often, wisdom is mistaken for the intellect, the knowledge we gather from reading or studying, but wisdom is the intelligence you bring to this world at birth, in the form of pure attention. If you have held on to that pure attention, as Einstein and other spiritual masters did, your wisdom will last until you die, and you will have navigated your life peacefully. Throughout this book, I refer to our wisdom as inner peace, since it is much easier to understand through our minds.

Self-check

I trust that I've cleared your pathway to wisdom through two different approaches. Suppose you are a philosopher; you go through a series of transformations to get there, like the life cycle of a butterfly changing its body in four stages. If the quality of a sage is prominent in you, you will transcend directly to inner peace, like a tadpole changing to a frog. Either way, with the help of those practices I introduced, you should be able to gain wisdom and dwell in your true self for the rest of your life. Please examine within and confirm that you had that experience of your true self. Check yourself and see whether you have that ability. If so, you should feel pleasantness and have an effortless, serene smile on your face.

Yet, instead of exploring within, many people seek happiness from outside. In the pursuit of happiness, most of us look for satisfaction from accumulating material things, as well as the opinions of others. It is a fundamental mistake in pursuing happiness to believe that satisfaction is happiness; it is a never-ending exercise. As mentioned, satisfaction depends on our perceptions. Since our perceptions change from one experience to another, we are never completely satisfied with any situation. The truth is that we create our own worlds with many thoughts, memories, perceptions, interpretations, judgments, and beliefs. They are all accumulated from external sources. Hence, we live in misery and chaos with a self-image created by others' commands and can never be satisfied. Our desire for worldly satisfaction obscures our true happiness. In other words, we act upon others' opinions and the speculations of our minds. We are in the chaos created by the enslaved mind, which tries to make us someone we are not: our flimsy self-image—*our fictional character*.

Since we live in a fictional character, we discriminate against everything to protect our self-image. That is the fundamental mistake obscuring true happiness. When we set aside all discrimination, including gender, we open our hearts to inner peace and true happiness. We can open our hearts using either the philosophers' or the sages' approach, which is the only difference we inherit at birth. With either of those approaches, we need to elevate our pure attention to the noble heart to experience our true selves. Our wisdom is knowing that and living with it.

I hope you now recognize your inner peace and see your mind as an independent faculty, distinct from your heart. If not, I urge you to do the self-checks throughout this expedition to reaffirm who you truly are. Then experience true happiness using the practices herein and learn to recognize your heart's inherent nobility. That profound experience will be the key to becoming a great sage or philosopher, a bearer of wisdom to live in your true self. With your reading and practice so far, you should have experienced your true self for at least a fraction of a second. This will blossom inner peace and allow you to comprehend the reality of this world. That is my vow to you!

As discussed, this is the way of all great philosophers and sages. We have examined those who shared their experiences of inner peace in ancient, medieval, and present times. My intention was to provide enough evidence to convince you that true happiness is not a phenomenon beyond your reach; it is available right here and now for you to experience. I hope I succeeded.

If you have not settled into your true self, yet, I trust that you are nonetheless determined to become a better philosopher or sage to experience true happiness. When your mind is as calm as undisturbed water, your cognitive ability is at its most intense. Consequently, with an open heart, you can see the world as it is, just as you would see the undistorted reflection of trees, hills, and the sky on still waters. You will be the master of your thoughts, not a victim of your mind. You will notice disturbing thoughts and emotions like birds chirping through the silence of the dawn. They are not yours, just the mind's trick to distract you from experiencing true happiness. You can experience this by revisiting the practices by following the index at the end of the book.

When inner peace and stillness prevail, you can use your thinking power wisely and create many things. You can see the world's reality undistorted by your mind's tricks. You will experience true happiness and become valuable to the new peaceful world.

If you are a scholar, you may wonder why I did not use common words like consciousness, mindfulness, and meditation in the practices I introduced. I purposely did not use them because your abstract or preconceived interpretations of such words might obscure my message and hinder your precious experience.

If you are a regular meditator, you may think I missed out vital instructions about "controlling your thoughts" while meditating. This is a fundamental mistake most meditators make, and thinking about controlling your thoughts is another thought distracting your inner peace. That is why I left out any mention of disturbing thoughts within the practices I introduced to you.

Also, you may be curious why I did not give some examples and exercises that you can use to resolve troubling day-to-day situations in your life. I assure you that you do not need to memorize such things to use them in a chaotic situation, even if you manage to remember them at the time. The practices you do here give you the experience of inner peace that will stay with you forever. You do not have to remember it; with an upward surge, your inner peace experience will help you in any circumstance. This is a solution that fixes any life challenges. When you dwell in inner peace and do not cling to your self-image, all challenges and pleasures are just incidents outside your true self. Therefore, you will respond to any situation effortlessly rather than having to recall memories.

As we examined, many philosophers and sages have dwelled in inner peace from ancient times to this day, and most prevailing religions are fundamentally based on the same truth of true happiness. There is a commonality in their pathway—*the ancient path*—that they follow to get to that truth. I find many resemblances in the ancient path to the practices I have introduced here. Therefore, you do not have to change your faith to dwell in your true self and experience true happiness.

If you are a true follower of the core teachings of any peace-loving religion, faith, or belief, you should not have the slightest doubt in the wisdom buried beneath this present moment. I do not doubt that many spiritual teachers who teach wisdom through being in the present are noble masters. This writing is by no means to disagree with such teachings. Instead, I hope this will assist you in overcoming fundamental misinterpretations of the message of being in the present.

In many cases, the followers of great teachers think of the present moment as "Now" but do not truly experience it. The present is between the past and future; the "Now" is a concept created by the mind relative to the past and future. When you think about the Now, it becomes a perception that exists between the past and future rather than a reality. Hence, you need to go beyond that perception of "Now" to live in the present with your true self.

Once you dwell in your true self, inner peace—*wisdom*—your kindness is not for good deeds or merit, your compassion is not relative to others, and empathy does not advertise your good qualities. Also, the degree of love does not depend on the other person; all that is effortless, limitless, and valueless. Your kindness, compassion, empathy, and love stem from inner peace in you and me. Hence, there is nothing to compare with; it benefits you, me, and us equally.

Inner peace is like the ocean; individualities or self-images are glasses filled with ocean water. These glasses are made of different thicknesses as our self-images differ from the degrees of our egos. However, water will eventually return to the ocean when the glass breaks. Once that water is mixed with the ocean, you cannot trace it back to the water you had in your glass. You and I have no identity in the ocean of inner peace. Therefore, whatever you do has the same impact on me, and vice versa. When we set aside all our differences, including gender, we become our innate selves and share true happiness. When you see the universal nature of your noble heart, your compassion, empathy, and love for yourself and others are impeccably equal.

Therefore, when you interact with others at that deeper level, your eyes may well up, expressing your heart's noble nature and inner peace. If those teardrops are water in your glass, their salty taste testifies that they came from the universal ocean of inner peace.

We live with fictional characters so that we can interact with each other and create many things in the world to comfort or differentiate us. The mind is the forerunner in this endeavor, but our heart always longs for unity and peace. With pure attention, we can identify the mind and heart's true value to dwell in inner peace, experience true happiness, and usher in our unity. I hope you experience this firsthand through the practices in this book.

Once you dwell in inner peace, it will be evident to others as they recognize the change that has come over you. This underlying state of your noble heart will be reflected on your face with a serene smile. It will lead others to seek the same peace that enriches your life with health and well-being. Just as planets revolve around the sun, your inner peace will attract peace-loving hearts around you. They, too, recognize their true selves — *inner peace* — and serve as the nucleus for others. And so inner peace will radiate from one to the other to create many peaceful souls, ensuring global peace. With that, we can evolve into a civilization that reveres peace and wisdom, a peace-loving world with unity. Many ancient civilizations prospered, enjoyed a peaceful lifestyle, and lived harmoniously. Therefore, this inner exploration to go beyond our self-image is a path used in ancient times — *the ancient path*. More people are discovering this ancient path and benefiting from it better than before. We are on the verge of evolving into an awakened civilization. Since you recognized your noble heart and experienced your true self, I trust you will vow to support global peace!

Index of Practices

References

1. Einstein, Estate of Albert, Selected and Edited by Helen Dukes and Banesh Hoffmann. *Albert Einstein: The Human Side*. Oxfordshire: Princeton University Press, (2013).

2. Hanh, Thich Nhat. *Peace Is Every Step: The Path of Mindfulness in Everyday Life*. New York: Bantam Books, (1991).

3. Isaacson, Walter. *Einstein: His Life and Universe*. New York: Simon & Schuster Inc, (2007).

4. Karmapa XVII. *The Heart Is Noble: Changing the World from the Inside Out*. Boston: Shambhala, (2013).

5. Sadhguru. *Inner Engineering: A Yogi's Guide to Joy*. New York: Penguin Random House LLC, (2016).

6. Singer, Michael A. *The Untethered Soul: The Journey Beyond Yourself*. Oakland: New Harbinger Publications and Noetic Books, (2007)

7. Tolle, Eckhart. *A New Earth: Awakening to Your Life's Purpose*. New York: PLUME, a member of Penguin Group USA Inc., (2006).

8. Tolle, Eckhart. *The Power of Now: A Guide to Spiritual Enlightenment*. Vancouver: Namaste Publishing Inc., (1997).

9. Nondual Consciousness: A Dialogue between Rupert Spira and Swami Sarvapriyananda, December 11, (2020). YouTube Video, Uploaded by Vedanta New York. Available at https://youtu.be/YhYKqblybXs ,(Accessed on November 30th, 2022)

10. Csanyi, Edvard, *Nikola Tesla: Everything is The Light*, (September 12, 2012) 1899, Interview with Nikola Tesla, Electrical-Engineering-Portal.com, Available at https://electrical-engineering-portal.com/nikola-tesla-everything-is-the-light. (Accessed on September 30th, 2022)

About the Author

N. T. (Nandasena Tellambure) Hettigei is a spiritual teacher, writer, and self-publisher who has shared his true happiness experience with others for the last three decades.

His life journey started in a rural village in Sri Lanka. He has navigated through personal and professional challenges in Sri Lanka, New Zealand, and the United States and attributes his success to inner peace. He is a retired certified public and chartered accountant—CPA and ACA—and an IT audit—CISA—and security professional—CISSP. He gave up his earlier career to fulfill the aspiration of sharing his experience of inner peace.

Since his teens, he has been a beacon on the ocean of inner peace and shared his firsthand experience in a small group setting and remote teaching and discussions. This sharing spread across many societies, such as group sittings with ordained monks in Stokes Valley Buddhist Monastery in New Zealand to spiritual seeker groups in Minneapolis, Minnesota, and Mesa, Arizona, in the United States and Sri Lanka.

He self-published "Are you a Philosopher or a Sage" in 2009 and "Explore Within" in 2019, with a new edition in 2022, which are the foundation for this book.

From the Author

Thank you for reading *Beyond Our Self-Image* to experience your true self. I sincerely hope you experience true happiness with the help of the practices I introduced in this book and commit to becoming a valuable member of this awakening world. Please share your experience with others, and feel free to add your book review to your favorite online site to spread inner peace.

Also, if you want to connect with others following the same path, visit www.ancientpath.org, which I formed in 1992, at the dawn of the internet, to promote world peace. Since then, I have noticed many initiatives, organizations, and spiritual teachers leading this effort online. You can see some of my recommendations in this space on this website.

I wish you true happiness!

Sincerely,

N.T. Hettigei

O-BOOKS

SPIRITUALITY

O is a symbol of the world, of oneness and unity; this eye
represents knowledge and insight. We publish titles on
general spirituality and living a spiritual life. We aim to
inform and help you on your own journey in this life.
If you have enjoyed this book, why not tell other readers
by posting a review on your preferred book site?

Recent bestsellers from O-Books are:

Heart of Tantric Sex
Diana Richardson
Revealing Eastern secrets of deep love and intimacy to Western
couples.
Paperback: 978-1-90381-637-0 ebook: 978-1-84694-637-0

Crystal Prescriptions
The A-Z guide to over 1,200 symptoms and their healing crystals
Judy Hall
The first in the popular series of eight books, this handy little
guide is packed as tight as a pill bottle with crystal remedies for
ailments.
Paperback: 978-1-90504-740-6 ebook: 978-1-84694-629-5

Shine On
David Ditchfield and J S Jones
What if the aftereffects of a near-death experience were undeniable? What if a person could suddenly produce high-quality paintings of the afterlife, or if they acquired the ability to compose classical symphonies? Meet: David Ditchfield.
Paperback: 978-1-78904-365-5 ebook: 978-1-78904-366-2

The Way of Reiki
The Inner Teachings of Mikao Usui Frans Stiene
The roadmap for deepening your understanding of the system of Reiki and rediscovering your True Self.
Paperback: 978-1-78535-665-0 ebook: 978-1-78535-744-2

You Are Not Your Thoughts.
Frances Trussell
The journey to a mindful way of being, for those who want to truly know the power of mindfulness.
Paperback: 978-1-78535-816-6 ebook: 978-1-78535-817-3

The Mysteries of the Twelfth Astrological House
Fallen Angels
Carmen Turner-Schott, MSW, LISW
Everyone wants to know more about the most misunderstood house in astrology — the twelfth astrological house.
Paperback: 978-1-78099-343-0 ebook: 978-1-78099-344-7

WhatsApps from Heaven
Louise Hamlin

An account of a bereavement and the extraordinary signs —
including WhatsApps — that a retired law lecturer received from
her deceased husband.

Paperback: 978-1-78904-947-3 ebook: 978-1-78904-948-0

The Holistic Guide to Your Health & Wellbeing Today
Oliver Rolfe

A holistic guide to improving your complete health, both inside
and out.

Paperback: 978-1-78535-392-5 ebook: 978-1-78535-393-2

Cool Sex
Diana Richardson and Wendy Doeleman

For deeply satisfying sex, the real secret is to reduce the heat, to
cool down. Discover the empowerment and fulfilment of sex with
loving mindfulness.

Paperback: 978-1-78904-351-8 ebook: 978-1-78904-352-5

Creating Real Happiness A to Z
Stephani Grace

Creating Real Happiness A to Z will help you understand the
truth that you are not your ego (conditioned self).

Paperback: 978-1-78904-951-0 ebook: 978-1-78904-952-7

A Colourful Dose of Optimism
Jules Standish
It's time for us to look on the bright side, by boosting our mood
and lifting our spirit, both in our interiors, as well as in our closet.
Paperback: 978-1-78904-927-5 ebook: 978-1-78904-928-2

Readers of ebooks can buy or view any of these bestsellers by
clicking on the live link in the title. Most titles are published in
paperback and as an ebook. Paperbacks are available in
traditional bookshops. Both print and ebook formats are available
online.

Find more titles and sign up to our readers' newsletter at
www.o-books.com

Follow O books on Facebook at **O-books**

For video content, author interviews and more, please subscribe to our YouTube channel:

O-BOOKS Presents

Follow us on social media for book news, promotions and more:

Facebook: O-Books

Instagram: @o_books_mbs

Twitter: @obooks

Tik Tok: @ObooksMBS